GW00497043

THE
AIR MINISTRY
SURVIVAL GUIDE

THE
AIR MINISTRY
SURVIVAL GUIDE

MICHAEL JOSEPH
an imprint of
PENGUIN BOOKS

MICHAEL JOSEPH

UK | USA | Canada | Ireland | Australia
India | New Zealand | South Africa

Michael Joseph is part of the Penguin Random House group of companies
whose addresses can be found at global.penguinrandomhouse.com

Penguin
Random House
UK

Desert Survival
First published by the Air Ministry 1952
Published in Penguin Books 2017

Jungle Survival
First published by the Air Ministry 1950
Published in Penguin Books 2017

Arctic Survival
First published by the Air Ministry 1953
Published in Penguin Books 2017

Sea Survival
First published by the Air Ministry 1953
Published in Penguin Books 2017

This collection first published as *The Air Ministry Survival Guide* by Michael Joseph 2018

001

The moral right of the author has been asserted

Printed and bound in Great Britain by Clays Ltd, Elcograf S.p.A.

A CIP catalogue record for this book is available from the British Library

HARDBACK ISBN: 978–0–241–36133–7

www.greenpenguin.co.uk

CONTENTS

DESERT

SURVIVAL

AIR MINISTRY PAMPHLET 225

DESERT SURVIVAL

INTRODUCTION

1. The word "desert" invariably produces in one's mind a picture of large, dry, barren tracts of land, hot in the daytime and cool at night, where the problem of survival is one of the first magnitude.

2. When it is realized that there is at least one desert in each continent of the world, it will be appreciated that this problem of survival is a very real one in the lives of those who fly. Approximately one-fifth of the world's land area is composed of desert, while the population of these areas amounts to less than one-twentieth of the total world population.

3. The aim of this pamphlet is to provide you with the necessary information to enable you to survive if you have to make a forced landing or parachute descent in the desert. You are urged to read it and thoroughly acquaint yourself with its contents, especially if you are operating over such terrain—it may save your life.

PRINCIPAL DESERTS OF THE WORLD

4. There are more than fifty important deserts in the world, the areas of which range from 300 to 3,000,000 square miles. The larger of these are well-known: Sahara (3,000,000 sq. mls.); Libyan (650,000 sq. mls.); Arabian (500,000 sq. mls.); Gobi, Mongolia (400,000 sq. mls.); Rub al Khali, part of the Arabian Desert (250,000 sq. mls.); and the Kalahari, Bechuanaland (200,000 sq. mls.).

5. The deserts with the most extreme climates are: the Sahara of North Africa; the Middle-Eastern deserts of Arabia, Iran and Iraq; parts of the Gobi in Mongolia; and the narrow strip along the coasts of Peru and Northern Chile. The Great Sandy Desert in Western Australia (160,000 sq. mls.), and the Mohave of the Southwestern United States and Northern Mexico (13,500 sq. mls.), are not "extreme" deserts, but they contain large waterless tracts which can present serious survival problems to aircrew.

DESERT CHARACTERISTICS

6. All deserts have certain things in common. Scarcity of water and great extremes of temperature are the outstanding characteristics. Rainfall is scarce though in parts of the Middle East it may be heavy during the winter. Surface water is absent over great areas for months at a time. Desert areas are generally cloudless, and high winds prevail over the larger ones for much of the year, with resulting serious sand and dust problems. Plant, animal, and human life is sparse and concentrated near the water sources. These oases, with their date groves and garden patches, may support up to 1,000 people per square mile. Large parts of the deserts however, are practically lifeless for long periods.

Surface Conditions

7. Deserts have various surfaces. Only a small part of them consists of soft sand (the popular conception of a desert). About a tenth of the Sahara is sandy, the greater part being a flat, barren, gravel plain from which the wind has blown the sand away and piled it up in the low-lying areas where the dunes are to be found. There are also mountainous areas, such as comprise the perimeter of the Arabian peninsular, varying in height from 6,000 to 12,000 feet. Other types of surface are plains dotted with sparse grass and thorny bushes (as in the Kalahari), mud flats and lava flows. There are lakes in some deserts, but permanent desert lakes with no outlets are salt lakes.

Climate

8. The temperature range in the extreme desert regions is considerable—hot days may be followed by freezing nights, the temperature dropping by as much as 50 to 70 degrees Fahrenheit. The following examples will serve to illustrate this point. At Habbaniya, in Iraq, the maximum and minimum temperatures recorded during the month of July are 123 deg. F. and 60 deg. F. respectively, while in January maximum and minimum recordings are 79 deg. F. and 16 deg. F., thus giving an annual variation of 107 deg. F. In the Western Sahara, the annual variation is very similar, ranging from a maximum of 125 deg. F. to a minimum of 22 deg. F. Sun temperatures during the hot season

often exceed these figures and have been known to reach 180 deg. F. The coldest desert is the Gobi, where the yearly absolute range is from 110 deg. F. in the summer to −40 deg. F and even −50 deg. F. in the winter, although the daily variation in temperature is less than that of the Sahara, being 25 deg. F. to 35 deg. F.

9. The following table is extracted from the meteorological data available at Habbaniya over a period of 14 years, and may be taken as typical of the Middle-Eastern deserts:—

RAINFALL AND TEMPERATURE RECORDS— HABBANIYA

1935-1949

	RAINFALL				TEMPERATURE			
	Mean Rainfall	Highest M'thly	Lowest M'thly	Highest in 24 hrs.	Mean Maximum	Mean Minimum	Highest	Lowest
	mm.	mm.	mm.	mm.	°F.	°F.	°F.	°F.
JANUARY	21.2	60.2	Trace	30.5	60.3	39.1	79	16
FEBRUARY	15.8	32.3	0.6	20.6	65.1	42.0	87	24
MARCH	24.1	83.1	0.1	28.5	75.0	47.9	97	27
APRIL	8.4	20.2	Trace	13.2	85.3	57.3	106	38
MAY	2.6	14.5	Trace	9.2	98.2	67.8	116	50
JUNE	Nil	Trace	Nil	Trace	106.7	73.2	120	60
JULY	Nil	Trace	Nil	Trace	111.6	77.9	123	69
AUGUST	Nil	Trace	Nil	Trace	111.7	76.7	122	67
SEPTEMBER	0.1	0.5	Nil	0.5	104.4	69.5	119	52
OCTOBER	2.5	20.8	Nil	15.2	92.4	61.3	107	42
NOVEMBER	17.6	39.8	Trace	24.3	76.4	51.0	95	33
DECEMBER	22.7	77.5	Trace	28.2	63.1	41.9	79	20

PRE-FLIGHT PRECAUTIONS

10. A thorough knowledge of the conditions likely to be encountered by a crew following an emergency descent into the desert, and adequate preparations at base are essential for survival. Before each flight, carefully check all emergency equipment in the aircraft, and personal survival equipment, and ensure that all items are serviceable. Immediately replace any that are missing or have deteriorated (see A.P. 1182C, Vol. 1 for scale of equipment). Remember that WATER is the first essential—your life depends on your water supply in the desert, so carry all the water you possibly can. If you have more equipment than you can carry, sacrifice anything but water. If the weight allowance of your aircraft is small (10 lbs. or less) put all of it into water. Only if you feel that you are carrying enough water, and if you have weight allowance left, should you pack food, emergency equipment, etc. The standard contents of the emergency packs may be modified to suit individual needs and local conditions. This should not be done on your own initiative, however, as it is dangerous with certain types of packs, such as those fitted in ejection seats.

11. The following items, in addition to water, should be carried if possible: heliograph, signal pistol and cartridges or flares, a small reliable compass, maps (indicating roads and sources of water if possible), tinted flying goggles or sun glasses, head covering, knife, matches, salt tablets, a minimum of concentrated emergency rations, first aid kit, anti-burn cream, torch, warm clothing (for use at night), and a pair of strong boots. A useful maxim to bear in mind is "always fly in the boots in which you intend walking home".

12. Your parachute is invaluable as an item of survival equipment in the desert. The canopy will give you shelter from the heat of the sun during the day and protection against cold at night. The pack itself can be modified to provide a knapsack, while the shroud lines will be found useful for many purposes.

13. Remember that if you are compelled to bale out, much of the equipment stowed in the aircraft will be lost to you. Make a point of carrying on your person some of the smaller items,

particularly a heliograph and signal flares. Failure to do this may jeopardize your chances of survival.

14. Make sure that you thoroughly know the emergency signals procedure and the rescue facilities available in the area over which you intend to fly. Proper use of these facilities will enable the rescue co-ordination centre to initiate search action promptly and limit the area of uncertainty.

15. Learn all you possibly can about the conditions you are likely to encounter in your particular area. Find out about the inhabitants, whether they are friendly or not, their customs, etc. Make a point of talking to crews who have had personal experience of desert survival—they will probably be able to give you some useful hints, and you may profit by their mistakes.

ACTION IN AN EMERGENCY

16. The captain of the aircraft should take immediate signals action if there is any danger, or possibility of danger, so that the ground station may be informed of the situation. These messages can always be cancelled if the emergency passes, but if omitted the aircraft may disappear without trace, making search action and subsequent rescue considerably more difficult.

17. When it becomes impossible or inadvisable to continue the flight two courses of action are open to you—a forced landing or a parachute descent. Over the desert a forced landing is preferable, as not only will the aircraft provide you with shelter and many items of emergency equipment, but will be a conspicuous landmark for searching aircraft. So try and stay with the aircraft and bring it down if possible. If the emergency is caused by lack of fuel, you should attempt a landing while you still have enough power to locate a suitable area and carry out the approach and subsequent crash landing.

18. In certain areas the prevailing wind direction can be determined by the formation of sand dunes which usually run approximately at right angles to it. These "sand seas" should be avoided if possible and a landing made on level ground, but if this is not feasible, and you have the choice of landing into wind or parallel

to the dunes, land across wind and parallel to the dunes. Avoid salt pans and wadis. Bear in mind the task of your rescuers, who may have to reach you by land rescue teams, and try to keep clear of areas which are impassable to them. Always try to bring your aircraft down near water sources or well-defined tracks, so that your chances of survival and rescue may be increased. A surface wind of any strength will be indicated by blowing dust. Landings should be made with the undercarriage retracted, even though the surface of the area chosen appears to be level and free from obstructions; it may be too soft to support the wheels, resulting in the aircraft turning over onto its back. If the aircraft has a fixed undercarriage, or the undercarriage cannot be retracted, do not use brakes during the landing run unless to avoid obstacles.

19. If you are forced to bale out, observe the descent of the aircraft and make your way to the wreckage if it is within reasonable distance. Even a wrecked aircraft is conspicuous from the air and will yield useful emergency equipment, so use it as a rendezvous for your crew.

IMMEDIATE ACTIONS AFTER LANDING

20. Leave the aircraft as soon as it has come to rest, taking with you as much water as you can and, if possible, your parachute and emergency packs. Stay well away from the aircraft until all danger of fire has passed.

21. There will be a great temptation to rush around trying to do everything at once. Try to resist this. *Take it easy.* Get into the shade immediately. Weigh up the situation calmly and decide on your course of action. There will be two things requiring your immediate attention—first aid and shelter.

First Aid

22. Attend promptly to all injuries. Remove all injured personnel into the shade as soon as possible. Follow the established first-aid practices:—

(a) *Wounds.* See that open wounds are dressed to prevent infection by dust and sand. Cut away clothing and don't handle the wound. Keep the wounded part at rest.

(*b*) *Fractures.* Fractured limbs should be immobilized by splints improvised from tight rolls of clothing or parts of the aircraft. (A hacksaw will be found useful for this purpose.) Don't remove clothing from the limb, but cut it away from wounds and dress them before splinting.

(*c*) *Hæmorrhage.* Control severe bleeding by applying a tourniquet between the injury and the heart. Release the tourniquet for half a minute every fifteen to twenty minutes.

(*d*) *Shock and Internal Injury.* Should be treated by keeping the person lying down and warm. If conscious, a hot drink can be given, provided the injury is not abdominal.

(*e*) *Sprains.* Bandage the injured part and keep it at rest until it can be moved without great pain. If swelling increases, remove the bandage to relieve the pressure and then rebind.

(*f*) *Burns.* Don't open blisters. Use the anti-burn cream in the first-aid kit or make a saline solution with the salt tablets and apply a dressing soaked in the solution to the affected part. Don't change the bandage, and keep the burned part at rest.

(*g*) *Cessation of Breathing.* If an injured man has stopped breathing, pull his tongue forward and apply artificial respiration. Check for head injuries or fractured skull (indicated by unequal pupils or bleeding from the ears or into the skin around the eyes.) Be very careful in handling such patients.

Shelter

23. Natural shelter will be limited to the shade of cliffs or hills. During most of the year the inside of the aircraft will be unsuitable as a shelter in the daytime owing to the intense heat. Even at night in the summer, in some deserts, it will be untenable. Only during the winter months should it be used for this purpose.

24. If the erection of a permanent shelter calls for exertions that will increase the sweat rate, this should be delayed until the temperature has dropped sufficiently to enable the work to be undertaken in comfort and, if necessary, a temporary shelter should be rigged to provide shade in the meantime.

25. The best shelter from the sun is provided by the wing of the aircraft. If the aircraft is resting firmly on the ground, with no danger of movement in a strong wind, the most suitable shelter can be improvised by draping a parachute canopy from the trailing edge of the mainplane. The lower edge of the canopy

DOUBLE LAYER OF PARACHUTE DRAPED OVER AIRCRAFT WING PROVIDES GOOD SHADE

should be not less than two feet from the ground to allow the air to circulate freely, and both upper and lower edges should be firmly secured. To reduce heat and glare most effectively, two parachute layers should be used, allowing an air space in between.

26. If the aircraft is a low-wing type, and resting on soft sand, scoop away the sand from under the mainplane to increase the clearance. By doing so you will dig down to where the sand is several degrees cooler. In most deserts, at a depth of 30 inches the temperature is below 70° F.

SHADE SHELTER OF PARACHUTE CLOTH
USE DOUBLE LAYER FOR GREATER COOLNESS

27. Other types of shelter can be made from your parachute, dinghy apron, tarpaulins, or blankets, using sticks, rocks, or removable parts of the aircraft for supports. Always use a

double layer of material for added protection, and allow an air space round the bottom which can be closed at night for warmth. Such shelters must be firmly secured against the prevailing high winds. Beds should be raised off the ground for greater cooling effect.

28. The aircraft will afford shelter from the cold during winter nights, when the temperature may drop to freezing or below, and from the violent rainstorms which may occur in most deserts at some season. Failing this, your parachute again will be

PARACHUTE SHELTER FOR COLD WEATHER

invaluable in providing you with shelter. Erect it in the form of a bell tent, pegging the sides to the ground or using rocks to keep them down. In the rainy season, camp on high ground and dig a drainage trench round the base of your shelter, with a "lead-away" trench running down the slope to prevent an accumulation of water. Collect this water to supplement your water supply.

PLAN OF ACTION

29. As soon as possible after landing and attending to immediate personal needs, the situation should be carefully sized up and a plan of action decided after discussion between all crew members. This must be done at the outset, when you are sufficiently fresh mentally and physically to think clearly. Once you have made your decision, stick to it, even though it may later appear to be wrong—your capacity to reason will diminish as time passes.

30. Decision must be reached on the following items, and perhaps others, peculiar to a particular emergency:—

    (a) Decision to stay or travel.

    (b) Rationing of water and food.

    (c) Signals contact.

(d) Ground signals.

(e) Allocation of duties.

(f) Log keeping.

(g) Preparation of landing strip or dropping zone.

Decision to Stay or Travel

31. Whether to stay or travel is the most important item for consideration. On it largely depends your chances of survival. The decision rests with the captain of the aircraft and must be based on a careful estimate of the situation. Factors which will influence the decision are:—

(a) *Position.* Try to pinpoint your position by studying maps, landmarks, flight log, or even by astro. You must know where you are before you can decide intelligently whether or not to remain with the aircraft, and to plan your direction and duration of travel if you do decide to walk out. If you were on track, or if your position is along a recognized air or land route, your chances of rescue from your present position are good.

(b) *Radio Contact.* Were you able to establish radio contact and transmit a distress message before making your forced landing or baling out? Can you contact ground stations or other aircraft from your present position?

(c) *Equipment.* Prepare an inventory of your emergency equipment, removing all items that are likely to be adversely affected by heat from the inside of the aircraft and storing them in the shade. Decide whether you have enough water and food for a desert trek and the chances of replenishing your supplies en route. Travel requires more water and food than staying in the shade. Reference to the water table on page 21 will show you how far you can expect to travel on the water available. What items can be improvised from parts of the aircraft? Is your clothing and footwear adequate for walking?

(d) *Physical Condition.* Consider your physical condition and that of the other members of the crew and estimate your ability to endure travel. Are you capable of carrying the equipment you require for a trek? Remember that a gallon of water weighs 10 lbs. If any of the crew are injured you may have to send the two strongest men for help. Don't send one man alone if it can be avoided.

(e) **Weather.** Does the prevailing weather allow adequate visibility for search action?

32. The best advice is to stay with the aircraft for at least five days—your chances of rescue are greatest during this period. The advantages of this action are:—

(a) The aircraft is easier to locate from the air than persons travelling.

(b) The aircraft provides you with shelter, signalling aids, and other useful emergency equipment.

(c) You will avoid the difficulties and hazards of desert travel.

33. Experience has shown that most rescues have been made when crews have remained with their aircraft.

Before you make a decision, consider ALL the factors.

Rationing of Water and Food

34. Rationing of water and food should be instituted immediately. It is impossible to lay down any hard and fast rules about rationing, as the amount of the daily ration will depend on several factors: the quantity available, your position, the probable lapse of time before rescue, and the chances of replenishing your supply (largely dependent on the season of the year).

35. The minimum daily water requirement to maintain life in the desert is a variable quantity, depending on the range in temperature, the physical condition of the person, and the degree to which he can protect himself from exposure to sun and heat.

36. Study paras. 59 to 77 on water consumption and the accompanying water tables, so that you can determine your bodily

water requirements and relate them to the existing conditions. Conserve your supply by keeping it in the shade to avoid evaporation and refrain from smoking, especially during the heat of the day.

37. If your emergency pack contains one of the plastic drinking cups, the ration may be measured by reference to the ridged divisions, each of which represents approximately two fluid ounces (20 Fluid Ounces = 1 Pint). The tins of water contain 14 fluid ounces, or approximately two-thirds of a pint.

38. When drinking, the lips, mouth, and throat should be moistened before swallowing.

39. Food is of secondary importance to water and the quantity taken should be very much restricted in hot climates if the amount of your daily water ration is less than one pint. A man in good condition can live for long periods without food, if he has sufficient water. If the daily water ration is less than one quart, don't eat foods rich in fat which require a considerable amount of water for their digestion and for the elimination of waste products. The best foods to eat are those of the carbohydrate, or sugar and starch group, such as potatoes, fruits, and the sweets in the emergency flying rations, which require very little water for their digestion. Vary the quantity of food according to the amount of water available; if the water ration has to be decreased, the food ration must be decreased in proportion.

40. When you are located by search aircraft, do not assume that rescue is imminent and consume all your supplies. If the first contact is made at night the position obtained by the aircraft may be only approximate, and a further day search may be necessary to establish it with greater accuracy before the dispatch of rescue teams. It may be some time before these rescue parties can reach you, so continue with strict rationing until you are picked up.

41. All ration issues should be recorded in the log at the time of issue so as to avoid arguments later.

Signals Contact

42. The aircraft radio is your best rescue aid. Although its range on the ground will be considerably reduced, this can be improved by erecting a vertical aerial—it is more efficient than the horizontal aircraft aerial. If the set is serviceable, transmit an S.O.S. message as soon as possible, giving your position, if known. Intersperse your transmission with 20-second dashes to allow D/F stations to take your bearing, and always conclude with the time at which you propose to transmit again. Always listen out before transmitting to ensure that the frequency is reasonably clear. If no reply is received, switch off and call again at fixed intervals. Always conserve your batteries—transmissions should be kept as short as possible—and make certain that all other electrical circuits (lights, gunsights, etc.) are switched off. Batteries may, if necessary, be topped up by urinating in them. If there is no risk of fire through fractured pipelines, etc., run up the engine charging the generator during transmission and reception, if possible—you will get better signals and lengthen the life of your batteries. This will require sufficient R.P.M. to bring in the cut-out so that the generator takes over the load. It should also be remembered that ground running of engines in the desert quickly leads to overheating and engine temperatures must be carefully watched. Engines should be kept covered when not in use to prevent entry of sand and dust. Transmissions at night on the appropriate destress frequency will give you greater range and, owing to the drop in temperature, will not cause the engine to overheat so quickly.

43. When using the Radio Transmitter SCR 578 ("Gibson Girl") in the desert, bury the ground contact and wet it with urine to increase the sending range, otherwise the range will be only a few miles. Under ideal conditions during the rainy season in the desert the range should be about 50 miles. If the weather is not suitable for using the kite, the aerial should be payed out to its fullest length and attached to the highest part of the aircraft.

44. The transmitter should be operated for periods of 4 minutes, at intervals of about 10 minutes, but if a serviceable and accurate watch is available you should transmit for periods of at least 3 minutes starting at 15 and 45 minutes past each hour.

15

45. With the radio set to automatic transmission, signals take the following form:—

> Auto 1 Position—S.O.S. for 20 seconds followed by a continuous dash for 20 seconds.
>
> Auto 2 Position—S.O.S. for 20 seconds followed by 4-second dashes for 20 seconds.

46. As the Auto 2 Position is designed to operate the automatic alarm on surface vessels, transmissions in desert regions should normally be confined to the Auto 1 Position, unless it is estimated that the crash position is such that transmissions on the Auto 2 Position may be received by surface craft (e.g. along the coastal strip of North Africa). In such case the 4-minute period should consist of 2 minutes on the Auto 1 Position followed by 2 minutes on the Auto 2 Position.

47. If the crash position is known, this can be transmitted along with any other information on the Manual Position outside the above periods.

48. The Radio Transmitter T3180 ("Walter") should be used sparingly. The life of the battery will be drastically reduced in tropical conditions and in extreme cases may fall to eight hours or even less. As a general rule, "Walter" should be used only when it is known that aircraft are in the vicinity. If a single aircraft has made a forced landing in the desert, it is pointless to switch on "Walter" immediately unless the aircraft is on a recognized route frequented by other aircraft. Better to conserve "Walter's" life until other aircraft have been able to start search action.

49. The transmitter should be switched on for periods of 2 minutes at 5-minute intervals, and should be left switched on if aircraft are heard or are known to be in the vicinity.

Ground Signals

50. Try to make your position as conspicuous as possible from the air. Full use should be made of equipment and materials whose colours form a contrast with the natural surroundings. Signalling equipment should be ready for use immediately an aircraft is heard—delay may be fatal. The following are some of the more practical methods of attracting attention:—

(*a*) Engine cowlings, removed and placed upside down make good reflectors, also portions of a metal wing surface from which the camouflage has been scraped. Surfaces can be brightly polished with sand or gravel—the reflection will be very apparent from the air in daylight.

(*b*) Spread out the dinghies and parachutes if they are not needed for shade.

(*c*) Use the heliograph for signalling during the daytime. This is the most effective visual signalling method when the sun is shining, ranges of 20 miles having been achieved. Rear vision mirrors or polished food tins will also serve this purpose. Signalling by these means should be practised regularly so that there is no delay in focusing when an aircraft is sighted.

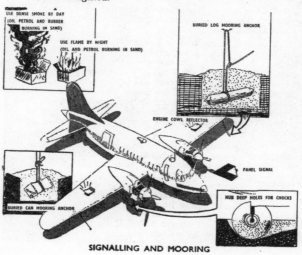

SIGNALLING AND MOORING

(*d*) Ground strips should be prominently displayed in the form of the signals given in the Ground/Air Emergency Code. In some areas it will be found possible to prepare signals by removing the top-soil and exposing the contrasting sub-soil.

(*e*) By night, if the landing lights are still intact, remove them from their housings and arrange them so that the

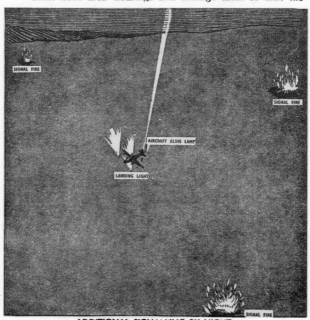

ADDITIONAL SIGNALLING BY NIGHT

reflectors are free to be pointed in all directions. They should be switched on only when an aircraft is heard in order to conserve the aircraft batteries. A vertical beam should not be used as this is not visible in certain conditions. An intermittent beam should be used in preference to a steady one. Aldis lamps may be similarly used.

(*f*) Use your signal cartridges sparingly. They should be used only at night when a aircraft is heard, or in reply to those fired by searching aircraft. Tracer ammunition and smoke bombs have also proved to be useful emergency signalling aids. Remember to keep all pyrotechnics dry and ready for instant use.

(*g*) At a safe distance from the aircraft, and on high ground if possible, lay three fires at least 100 feet apart in the form of a triangle. These may be kept burning continuously if adequate fuel is available, or prepared for use immediately an aircraft is heard or sighted. Use flame by night (burning petrol and oil in sand), and dense smoke by day—adding rubber (parachute cushions, electrical insulation, floor mats, etc.), or urine to produce steam.

Allocation of Duties

51. An allocation of duties, to be carried out when climatic conditions permit, is essential for the morale of the crew, helping to prevent those mental disturbances which are likely to arise in such situations and which are sometimes indicated by outbursts of temper or moroseness, as well as increasing the chances of rescue.

52. The captain may have to show firmness to ensure that the duties detailed by him are carried out, owing to a natural tendency to let discipline relax.

53. Among the duties allotted by the captain should be that of lookout or aircraft spotter. This is necessary to overcome the necessity of the whole crew being on the alert during the heat of the day. The lookout should have the various signalling devices readily available, and be positioned on the highest ground in the vicinity and near any signal fires that may have

been prepared so that there will be no delay in lighting them when an aircraft is heard or sighted. This duty should be limited to periods of one hour during the heat of the day.

54. The duty of issuing rations is solely that of the captain.

Log Keeping

55. A log should be started as soon as possible and kept throughout the whole period. The first entry should include all details of the emergency: nature of emergency; action taken; date, time, and position of landing or bale-out; names of crew and injuries sustained; weather conditions; equipment and rations available. Subsequent entries should contain details of rations issued, duties allotted, weather, crew morale and physical condition, aircraft sighted, and particulars of any preparations made.

56. The log need not necessarily be kept by the captain, provided he ensures that the correct entries are made. The duty could be delegated to the weakest member of the party, or possibly to an injured man, thereby helping him to overcome a possible feeling that he is a liability on the other survivors.

Preparation of Landing Strip or Dropping Zone

57. The possibility of preparing a suitable stretch of ground nearby for use as an emergency landing strip by rescue aircraft should not be overlooked. Obstructions should be removed and the area clearly marked by strips torn from parachutes. A landing T and the signal △ "Probably safe to land here", from the Ground/Air Emergency Code, should be prominently displayed.

58. A dropping zone for supplies should also be clearly indicated on a site adjacent to the camp to prevent them being dropped some distance away. The retrieving of supplies over any distance may well be a task beyond the capabilities of weakened survivors.

WATER

The Importance of Water

59. Water is the key to survival in the desert. Your life expectancy under emergency conditions is determined by the amount

of water available and also the degree to which you can protect your body from direct exposure to the sun and heat, thereby minimising bodily water loss through perspiration and evaporation.

60. The following desert water table shows the number of days of expected survival under two conditions: first, resting in the shade at all times, and second, walking at night and resting by day. It also shows the distances that can be covered.

DESERT WATER TABLE

Days of Expected Survival

Condition	Max. Daily Shade Temp. °F.	Total Available Water per Man (Quarts)					
		0	1	2	4	10	20
Resting in the shade at all times.	120	2½	2½	2½	3	3½	5½
	110	3½	3½	4	4½	6	8½
	100	6	6½	7	8½	11½	16
	90	8½	9½	10½	12½	18	27½
	80	10½	12	13	15½	23	35
	70	12	13	14½	17	24½	38½
	60	12	13	14½	17	25	38½
	50	12	13	14½	17½	25	38½
			1	2	4	10	
Walking only at night and resting in the shade by day. (Total mileage shown in brackets)	120	1 (25)	2½(25)	2½ (30)	3 (35)	3½ (40)	
	110	2½(25)	2½(25)	3 (30)	3½ (35)	4 (40)	
	100	3½(25)	4 (25)	4 (30)	5½ (35)	6½ (50)	
	90	6 (35)	6½(35)	6½ (40)	8 (55)	9½ (60)	
	80	8½(50)	9 (55)	9½ (60)	11½ (70)	14 (90)	
	70	9 (55)	9½(60)	11 (80)	12½(102)	16 (130)	
	60	9½(60)	10 (70)	11 (100)	13 (130)	17 (180)	
	50	9½(70)	10 (90)	11 (120)	13 (180)	17 (180)	

61. It will be seen from the table that absence or shortage of water, especially in the higher temperature ranges, severely limits the time of survival or distance travelled. Survival time is not appreciably increased until the available water per man is about four quarts.

Physiological Considerations

62. Water constitutes about 70 per cent. of body weight, so that, as the weight of the average man is about 154 lbs., the human body contains roughly 11 gallons of fluid. Only a maximum of 2½ gallons, or one-fifth, of this can be lost if the individual is to survive. The signs and symptoms of such dehydration are: 1 to 5 per cent. of body fluid lost (up to 4 pints)—thirst, vague discomfort, lack of appetite, flushed skin, impatience, sleepiness and sickness; 6 to 10 per cent. (5 to 9 pints)—dizziness, headache, laboured breathing, absence of salivation, indistinct speech and inability to walk; 11 to 20 per cent. (10 to 18 pints)—delirium, swollen tongue, inability to swallow, deafness, dim vision, numb and shrivelled skin. In the latter stages it will be noted that there is gross muscular weakness and mental capacity may be severely impaired, hence the importance of formulating your plan of action as early as possible and not deviating from it later.

63. It is obvious that, as far as possible, fluid loss should not be permitted to exceed about 8 pints if the survivor is to be kept in reasonably good condition.

64. The ideal use of water under desert survival conditions is to allow a slight negative balance (*e.g.* 3 to 4 pints) to accumulate, and then drink at the rate at which sweating is taking place. In this way there is little impairment in efficiency and no water will be wasted. When the available water supply is reduced to about a pint, this last pint may be used for wetting the mouth, but under hot desert conditions it will have little influence on the duration of survival. The estimation of a negative balance is difficult, but *a moderately severe sensation of thirst is a good indication.* For this reason some pamphlets have advised that no water should be taken during the first 24 hours. While this is good advice for survival at sea under most conditions and under moderate conditions on land, it could be dangerous if the temperature is very high or some work has to be undertaken, as it is quite possible to lose as much as 2½ gallons in that period by sweating.

65. *Individual minimum water requirements therefore depend on loss of water.* This water loss takes place in two ways: by evaporation through sweat, etc., and through the kidneys as urine. Both these losses consist of two parts; a small, steady amount of about $1\frac{1}{2}$ pints per day; and a variable amount, which in the case of the urine is the excess of intake over output (or overflowing of the body "reservoir"), and in the case of evaporation is proportional to the degree of activity of the individual and to the temperature.

66. An indication of the latter loss is that if the daily mean temperature exceeds 80 deg. F., walking at night instead of resting at all times increases the water requirement by $3\frac{1}{2}$ pints per 24 hours. Alternatively, an increase of daily mean temperature from 70 deg. F. to 93 deg. F., under resting conditions, increases the daily water requirement from $1\frac{3}{4}$ pints to 7 pints. While there are individual variations, in general, sweat loss is proportional to body weight and extreme variations are uncommon.

67. It is often stated that reduction in fluid intake will cause a reduction in the sweat rate. This has been shown to be without foundation. However, if more fluid is taken than is being lost by sweating, the excess will be excreted in the urine and thus lost to the individual.

68. Having obtained a slight degree of dehydration by the method previously outlined, the water should be rationed to the amount estimated to be lost by sweating under the existing conditions, taking into account the mean temperature and activity. When adequate water is available, there is no point in reducing the intake below the amounts shown in para. 69. Smaller amounts will only lead to progressive dehydration and loss of physical and mental efficiency.

69. The following figures are only approximate and assume rest in the shade at all times. In the desert the mean temperature can be taken as $15°$ F. below the daily maximum.

DAILY WATER REQUIREMENTS TO MAINTAIN WATER BALANCE

Mean Temp. deg. F.	Pints per 24 hrs.
95	9
90	$6\frac{1}{2}$
85	$4\frac{1}{2}$
80	$2\frac{1}{2}$
75	2

At a mean temperature of 65° F. or below (Temperate or Winter Desert Conditions) water loss is at the basal amount of $1\frac{3}{4}$ pints per 24 hours.

Average summer conditions in and near the Suez Canal Zone are represented by the 90° F. figure.

70. As these figures are for resting in the shade at all times, they are minimum requirements and under survival conditions will often be exceeded, so that an intake of this amount may not be enough to maintain water balance. If the available water supply is insufficient to maintain even the required minimum intake, then a progressive dehydration will take place. Other influencing factors will be the degree of protection that can be obtained from the sun and heat, and the individual activity.

71. Bearing in mind that the sweat loss when walking in the desert in a temperature of just over 100° F. is 2 pints per hour, it will be evident that there is not much future in trying to walk away from a forced landing when the sun is up during the summer. During the winter, of course, considerable distances may be covered.

72. Rationing of water is valuable for morale and to ensure that everyone gets a fair share, but it should not be more severe than indicated in para. 69 if the supplies are available. There is no point in drinking at any particular time and water should be taken at suitable intervals throughout the day. *It is a fallacy that water taken during the heat of the day is immediately lost due to an increase in sweat rate.*

73. Smoking will not increase your actual bodily need for water, but should not be encouraged as it will only lead to an uncomfortable dryness of the mouth. Chewing gum or sucking pebbles may help temporarily to relieve any such dryness, but they are not a substitute for water and will not help in maintaining the level of your body fluid.

74. It can now be seen that just as important as the rationing of water is the rationing of sweat. Keep in the shade at all times during the heat of the day. Work only at night. Keep your body and head well covered, not only as protection against the sun but also to minimize the evaporation of sweat, thereby gaining maximum cooling effect. This covering must be as light and as loose as possible so as to provide adequate ventilation, otherwise an increase in sweat rate will result.

Sources of Water

75. The possibility of replenishing your water supply should not be overlooked. This will largely depend on your location and the season of the year, but do not rely too much on finding water when determining the duration of your stay or travel. The only safe way is to carry with you the water that you need.

76. The following are some of the possible sources of water in desert regions:—

(a) *Wells and Water Holes*. Ensure that these are marked on your map beforehand. They are usually to be found along the caravan routes. As they may be quite deep, with the water level below easy reach, it is advisable to carry a length of light line for lowering a can or some suitable container. The small water holes in dry stream courses, or in other low places known to the natives, are often kept covered with a flat rock or sand and require a careful search for their location. Edges of ancient water holes are built up above their surroundings by accumulations of excrement around them. Look for these mounds.

(b) *Rain*. During the rainy season, rain traps should be erected to catch as much water as possible. Any piece of tarpaulin or dinghy apron can be suspended between four stakes, allowing the water to drain down and accumulate in the centre. An inflated dinghy will also serve this purpose.

(c) *Condensation*. During the cooler months some deserts are humid enough at night for dew to form. To collect this, scoop a shallow basin in the ground and line it with canvas, dinghy apron, or parachute. Over this, pile stones until the basin is filled. During the night the dew will collect on the stones and trickle down on to the lining. Metal parts of the aircraft will also collect dew. Engine cowlings should be removed and placed upside down to allow the moisture to accumulate. Dew should be collected at first light before evaporation takes place.

(d) *Dry Stream Beds and Gullies*. By digging at the lowest point of the outside of a bend in the bed of a channel, or the lowest point between dunes, a source of water may be found. If wet sand or mud is found, put it in a cloth and wring out the water.

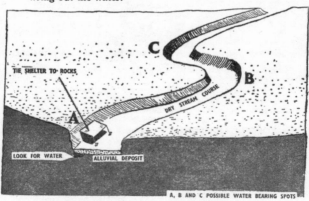

WATER AND SHELTER IN A DRY STREAM COURSE

(e) *Sandy Beaches*. The water first revealed by digging a hole just above the high-tide mark should be fit for drinking. Further digging only produces water which is too salty.

(*f*) *Desert Plants*. Some desert plants store water in their trunks, branches or roots. Such plants are found mainly along desert fringes in semi-arid terrain and near water holes. Avoid plants with milky sap—they are poisonous. The presence of vegetation is not always a sign that water is available. In the Middle East, for example, the palm is the only plant which indicates that water is close at hand.

Purification of Water

77. Water obtained by any of the methods previously outlined, or tinned water that may be tainted or suspect, should be purified before drinking by one of the following methods:—

(*a*) *Halazone Tablets*. Crush and dissolve one halazone tablet in each pint of water. Shake well and allow to stand one hour before drinking. If this is insufficient to produce a distinct smell of chlorine, add more tablets until the odour is present.

(*b*) *Boiling*. Boil the water for at least three minutes and allow any sediment to settle while cooling.

(*c*) *Iodine*. Add two or three drops of iodine to each quart of water and allow to stand for 30 minutes.

DONT DRINK UNPURIFIED WATER—it will only lead to dysentery.

DON'T DRINK ALCOHOL—it will cause nausea and increase thirst. It is dangerous to drink alcohol under such conditions and may even bring about convulsions.

DON'T DRINK URINE—it is poisonous and will decrease your resistance and increase your thirst.

SALT

78. Sweat contains salt as well as water, and the loss of this salt must be made good, otherwise you may suffer from heatstroke, heat exhaustion, or muscular cramps.

79. One of the ways in which a man gets used to hot climates is by replenishing the amount of salt lost in the sweat. This is particularly necessary during the first week, when maximum sweating is likely to occur.

80. Under normal living conditions enough extra salt can be absorbed with the food at mealtimes, but under survival conditions two or three salt tablets should be taken every day provided that an adequate supply of water is available.

FOOD

81. There is little animal or plant life in the true desert regions and you should never rely on replenishing your food supplies from these sources. When you reach an oasis you are no longer in the desert in the survival sense, for you have reached a populated area and your rescue is only a matter of time. However, food is less important than water. You can manage without food for several days with no ill effects.

82. Food spoils quickly in the desert. Tinned emergency rations should be opened only as needed and the contents eaten as soon as possible after the containers have been opened.

Animal Food

83. The presence of game animals depends primarily on the presence of water and cover, and there is little of either in the true desert. Look for animals at water holes, in low-lying areas where there is a greater chance of moisture, under rocks, and in bushes. They are more commonly seen at dusk or dawn than during the heat of the day. The most common animals are small rodents (rabbits, desert dogs, rats) and lizards. Rodents may be caught by finding their burrows and snaring them with a loop snare when they come out at dusk or dawn. Gazelles or antelopes may be found in the open desert and may be taken by a good shot with a rifle, but don't go chasing them or you may wander too far and become lost, or at least expend precious energy and water, all to no avail.

84. Animal food will be difficult to find in the Middle Eastern deserts, but in the Gobi herds of antelope numbering up to a hundred animals may be encountered: on the other hand you may strike areas where there are none at all. The most common forms of animal life in the deserts of Iran and Iraq are birds, such as partridge, quail, and bustard, which frequent the river beds and other water sources.

Plant Food

85. Edible plant food is rare in the desert. Grasses are edible, as are some of the wild plants or their roots that may be found along dry stream beds or around water holes, but they are unlikely to be palatable or possess any real nutritive value. If you are tempted to try any plant food, avoid those with a milky or coloured sap—they are poisonous—and eat only a small quantity. Wait eight hours and if there are no ill effects, such as vomiting or diarrhoea, repeat the dose and wait for a similar period. If there are still no ill effects, you can eat reasonable quantities with safety.

86. Palms, which are found near water holes, will provide food in the form of dates and the palm cabbage, a tender shoot which extends up from the top of the trunk at the point where the leaves spread out. It may be eaten raw or cooked.

CLOTHING

DESERT CLOTHING

87. Clothing is of the greatest importance in the maintenance of health in hot climates, as a protection against the sun, heat, thorns, and insect bites. It protects the body against excessive loss of fluid and salts by sweating, so that if you go around without a shirt much of the sweat may evaporate quickly without your notice. Keep your body and head covered during the heat of the day, otherwise you will very likely suffer from sunburn, heatstroke, or heat exhaustion.

Body

88. Light, loose-fitting clothes are best. The air space between the loose garment and the body acts as an insulator against the

heat of the sun. The natives have discovered this fact by experience and have adopted loose flowing robes. Sleeves should be kept loose and flapping. The legs should also be kept covered, and slacks worn in preference to shorts.

89. The stomach should be carefully protected both day and night. It is particularly susceptible to chill resulting from the drop in temperature at night, or to cooling by the evaporation of sweat. Such chilling may lead to acute diarrhoea or even dysentery. Do not sleep with the stomach uncovered: an improvised woollen band worn round the waist at all times will guard against this rapid chilling.

90. Owing to the extremes in temperature, the need for additional clothing will be felt at night. If warm clothing is not available, use your parachute to make a sleeping bag, wrapping several thicknesses round yourself cocoon fashion.

Head

91. It is particularly important to protect the head and back of the neck against direct exposure to the sun. A service cap provides safe protection against sunstroke, provided a piece of cloth is hung over the back of the head, neck, and shoulders.

CUT

HEADGEAR FASHIONED
FROM SEAT CUSHION

92. If you have no hat, protection can be obtained by improvising a seat cushion. The cushion should be slit open, and a piece of shroud line used as a chin strap to secure it on the head.

93. An alternative form of headgear, and one more suitable in hot climates, can be copied from the Arab headdress as follows:—

(a) Make a 4-foot square composed of several layers of parachute cloth.

(b) Make a double rope loop about the size of the crown of your head (size of hat band).

(c) Put a wadded handkerchief or cloth on top of your head. Fold the square of cloth diagonally and place it on top of the handkerchief; fasten in place by the loop of rope.

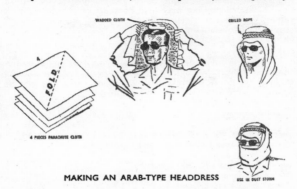

MAKING AN ARAB-TYPE HEADDRESS

94. This headdress has the additional advantage of affording protection for the face against swirling sand during sandstorms, when the tails of the covering can be tucked across the face. Failing this, an improvised face cloth should be tied over the lower part of the face.

Eyes.

95. Eyes must be protected against glare, both direct and reflected. Sun glasses or dark goggles must be worn throughout the day. Goggles have the advantage of protecting the eyes during sandstorms, but unless they are adequately ventilated may prove uncomfortable during the heat of the day.

96. If neither glasses nor **goggles** are available, a piece of cloth with slits cut for the eyes (just large enough to allow a penny to pass through) makes a good eyeshield. Smearing soot under the eyes helps to reduce glare.

CUT NARROW SLITS IN PIECE OF CLOTH
FOR IMPROVISED EYESHIELDS

Feet

97. The feet should be kept in good condition. This is very important, as on it may depend your return to safety. They should be inspected at frequent intervals and shoes should be removed when resting and emptied of sand.

98. Socks should be changed regularly. If you can wear two pairs of socks, the inside pair should be worn inside-out and the two pairs should be interchanged at intervals.

99. Thin soles can be reinforced by lacing on an outer sole improvised from rubber floor covering or tyre walls.

100. Unless you are wearing flying boots, you must try to prevent sand entering your shoes. Make a pair of puttees from strips of parachute cloth, covering an inch or two of the shoe tops and three inches of the legs. Slacks should be worn outside the puttees to maintain adequate air circulation.

PUTTEES OF PARACHUTE CLOTH
WILL KEEP SAND AND INSECTS
OUT OF SHOES

101. If you lose your shoes, or if they wear out, improvise a practical pair of sandals using floor covering or the rubber

IMPROVISED SANDAL

side-wall of a tyre for the soles and parachute cloth or canvas for the uppers and heel straps. The felt covering of the T3180, "Walter" Transmitter, will provide a comfortable inner sole.

General

102. If you are caught out in a sandstorm, button up your clothing tightly, fastening wrist bands and trouser bottoms. Cover the face with a cloth and lie down, back to wind. To avoid sand piling up around you, roll about from time to time.

103. Always inspect clothing carefully and shake it thoroughly before putting it on, to guard against spiders and scorpions.

FIREMAKING

104. Fires will be needed for warmth at night, especially during the winter months, and for signalling, cooking, and purifying water by boiling. A hot drink, even if it is only water, is a great morale raiser.

IMPROVISED STOVE USING PETROL

105. Provided oil and petrol are available from the aircraft, the problem of firemaking is simple. You can make a stove out of any metal container or by building stones in a small circle. Fill the container with sand drenched with oil, then add a little petrol and light with a match. Holes should be made at the

33

lower end to allow ventilation and round the top to let the flame and smoke out. Try to wall your fire in to concentrate the heat and provide a platform for your cooking pot. Never add petrol to a fire already started or even smouldering.

IMPROVISED STOVE TO BURN
OIL AND ANIMAL FAT

106. Lubricating oil will not burn directly, but you can use it for fuel with a wick arrangement. The wick can be made of rope, string, rag, or even a cigarette.

107. In and near oases, stems of palm leaves and similar wood will serve as fuel. Out in the open desert, use scrub or any dead vegetation. Dry roots will burn well—a small stick protruding out of the sand will often yield enough fuel to boil a can of water if the roots are dug out carefully.

108. Dried camel dung makes a good emergency fuel, burning with a smoky yellow flame.

109. Conserve your matches. Try to light a fire with just one match. If using a wood or scrub fire, always start in a small way and build up your fire gradually. Use small pieces of wood arranged in a low pyramid, with lint from unravelled cloth, rope, or first aid gauze bandage to start the fire. A few drops of petrol will make this kind of tinder catch very readily.

110. Fires can also be kindled without using matches. The flint and steel is one method, especially when petrol is available. A lens from a camera, binoculars, or reflector sight, can be used in bright sunlight to concentrate the sun's rays on tinder and start it burning. If the aircraft battery is serviceable, a spark can be produced by scratching together the bare ends of two wires connected to the battery.

111. Always build your fire on the leeward side of the aircraft or shelter.

NATIVES

112. In desert areas most habitations are along the coastal strips or near the water holes and oases. In most deserts there are also wandering tribes, following the trails and caravan routes from water hole to water hole.

113. Learn as much as possible about the natives in the area in which you have to operate. Study their habits, religious customs and manners—it may be of use to you some day. They are usually a proud and independent people, with a way of life and a culture that they value highly. Their habits may appear peculiar to you, but do not scoff at them. Remember that to them *you* are the strange ones. Be especially careful not to offend them.

114. With few exceptions natives are friendly. They know the country, its trails, food and water sources, and can be the means of your being speedily returned to civilization. In short, they are your best help—but it all depends on how you approach them.

115. Hostile parties may be encountered in certain areas (*e.g.* Southern Arabia). Be on your guard against them. If you do meet this type of native, then "blood chits", money and great tact may see you through.

116. When dealing with natives the following rules should be observed:—

(*a*) Don't rush matters. They may be shy and unapproachable at first. Show courtesy and patience. A gift and a friendly manner will help to open negotiations.

(*b*) Always deal with the recognized headman or chief.

(*c*) Ask for help—don't demand it.

(*d*) If you make a promise, keep it.

(*e*) Respect personal property. Always make some kind of payment for what you receive.

(f) Avoid things that are taboo, such as native women, certain animals, etc.

(g) Leave a good impression. Other crews may need their help later and you can go a long way to making things easier for them by your manner and appreciation of hospitality and help.

ALWAYS BE TACTFUL, PATIENT, AND HONEST.

DESERT AILMENTS

117. Protection of health is of the first importance under survival conditions. Whether you stay with the aircraft or decide to walk out, your physical condition will have a lot to do with your coming out safely.

118. The following are the chief desert illnesses. With the exception of the last, all are attributable to excessive exposure to sun and heat and can be guarded against by keeping the body and head protected and by remaining in the shade during the heat of the day.

(a) *Heat Cramps.* Usually the first warning of heat exhaustion. The cramps usually occur in the muscles which are actually in use, probably the abdomen, arms, and legs. Caused by lack of body salt after a person has been sweating a great deal, especially if extra salt has not been taken. Symptoms are shallow breathing, vomiting, and dizziness. Treatment is to move the person into the shade and give salt dissolved in water (two tablets to a quart) until the cramps are relieved.

(b) *Heat Exhaustion.* Caused by exposure to high temperature and humidity, resulting in loss of body fluids through excessive sweating. May occur without direct exposure to the sun. The face is pale and the skin cold and sweating. Accompanied by nausea, dizziness, weakness, and perhaps cramps. The pulse is weak and the person may become delirious or unconcious. Treat as for heat cramps and keep the person at rest.

(c) **Heatstroke.** The third and most serious result of over-exposure to the direct rays of the sun, although it can affect a person who has been under cover. Symptoms are a hot, dry skin; sweating stops; the face is flushed and feverish; temperature rises and the pulse rate becomes fast and strong; there is severe headache and often vomiting. Unconsciousness may follow. Treatment is to lower the body temperature as soon as possible. Lay the person in the shade, with head and shoulders slightly raised. Remove outer clothing and cool the body by wetting the underclothing with water and by fanning. If water for cooling is not available, scoop out a trench in the sand and place the person in the bottom. Rig a sun awning, leaving an air space for ventilation. As soon as consciousness returns, give water with salt tablets added (two tablets to a quart). When the temperature is back to normal, replace clothing and keep warm to prevent a chill.

(d) **Sunburn.** A very painful and unnecessary ailment caused by excessive exposure of the body to the sun, particularly when not acclimatized. It can be dangerous: if more than two-thirds of the body is affected, sunburn is likely to prove fatal. Treat affected parts with sunburn cream.

(e) **Sore Eyes.** Excessive exposure of unprotected eyes to direct sunlight, glare, or dust particles, will result in them becoming sore. Treat with boracic ointment and bandage lightly. In the absence of a suitable ointment a damp bandage should be applied.

(f) **Constipation or Difficult Urination.** Can be expected with a shortage of food and water and should not give cause for alarm. Indiscriminate use of laxative tablets will also lead to an increase in urine, with consequent loss of body fluid and salt.

119. Desert sores may develop when the skin is broken under survival conditions. All wounds, however trivial, should be promptly treated with antiseptic ointment, if available, and covered with a sterile bandage.

120. If it is decided that the chances of rescue from the crash position are remote and the only hope of survival is to walk out, then careful plans must be made before setting out on what may well be a journey of considerable duration. A desert trek is not to be embarked on lightly, and should be undertaken only if it is certain that the objective can be reached on the water supply available. Do not underestimate the difficulties that will be encountered or overestimate your physical condition.

121. It may not be advisable for the entire crew to attempt the journey ; it may be better for say two members to set out for help, the remainder awaiting rescue with the aircraft. This will depend on the situation and the supplies available, especially water. One advantage of this method is that you have a double chance of coming through.

Preparations for Travel

122. Check all available equipment and decide which items to take with you. Don't overload—the total weight of equipment carried by each person should not exceed 35 lbs. As water will be your chief requirement, it should comprise the greater part of this weight allowance (1 Gallon = 10 lbs.); the remainder should consist of signalling equipment and some material from which you can improvise a shelter, preferably a piece of parachute canopy. Other smaller necessities are a compass, maps, pencil and paper, knife, salt and halazone tablets, sunglasses, first aid kit, torch, and of course a watch. A bare minimum of food should be taken, especially if you are short of water. It may be possible to improvise a walking stick from some part of the aircraft structure.

123. A good rucksack can easily be made from a seat-type parachute by trimming it and cutting off the excess harness and back pad. Other types of parachute packs can be modified in this way with a little thought and ingenuity.

124. A lighter, but less comfortable, pack can be made by simply wrapping the equipment in the canopy and securing it by the harness straps or rigging lines. Always try to make the pack sit as high as possible on the shoulders so that it will not bang in the small of the back at every step.

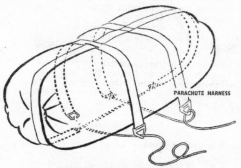

PARACHUTE HARNESS

IMPROVISED ROLL-TYPE PACK

125. Before leaving the aircraft, destroy all classified documents and any secret equipment. Leave a note in a prominent position, detailing the members of the party, direction in which travelling and objective, and the date set out. Your route should be marked if possible, and a log and sketch map maintained.

Hints on Travel

126. During the hottest part of the year travel should be undertaken only at night, although considerable distances may be covered in daylight in the winter months. A double awning should be made with a parachute canopy to provide shade during the heat of the day. Rest in the shade at all times and get as much sleep as possible. Remove shoes and socks when resting.

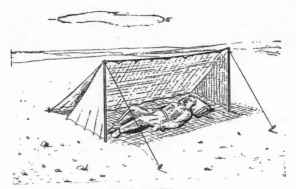

LIGHT SHELTER

127. Don't hurry. Adjust your pace to that of the slowest man and use a long, slow gait rather than short, quick steps. Follow the easiest route and avoid soft sand areas and rough terrain as much as possible. A good idea is to make a compulsory halt for ten minutes every hour. Shoes should be emptied of sand at frequent intervals.

128. When marching at night, map reading and pinpointing may not be easy. Even on clear nights there is a lack of perspective which can have serious consequences. A drop of fifty or sixty feet may appear to be only a slight dip. A torch in these circumstances is a necessity, and it is advisable for the party to walk in single file.

Choosing the Route

129. Your position should be accurately determined and marked on the map before setting out. When deciding your objective, it is better to choose one that is easy to find—*e.g.* a coast or road which can then be followed until habitation is reached—rather than a specific objective such as a settlement or oasis. In this

way you can allow for a greater margin of error in your direction. If a definite objective is decided upon, note any prominent adjoining feature, perhaps a road leading to it or a range of hills, to help you in locating it.

130. If you have come down in an area in which there are trails, these will lead you to water. Follow the arrow-head formed by converging trails to reach the nearest water hole.

131. Once you have decided on your objective, *stick to it.*

How to Determine and Maintain Direction

132. A compass is provided in the survival pack to enable you to determine direction. If this is not available, use the compass from the aircraft but remember to remove the compensating magnets. Allow for magnetic variation as shown on your maps.

133. Even without a compass it is possible to determine direction. If your objective is a large one, such as a coast-line, the simple fact that the sun rises in the east and sets in the west should be sufficient indication of your direction of travel. Actually the sun rises due east and sets due west only on March 21st and September 23rd—the equinoxes. If you wish to estimate the point of sunrise with greater accuracy, the following table will give you the angle of sunrise from true north at different times of the year and at different latitudes.

SUNRISE TABLE

DIRECTION IN WHICH SUN RISES — DEGREES EAST OF TRUE NORTH
Direction measured when top of sun just shows above horizon.

LATITUDE	MAR. 21	MAY 5	JUNE 22	AUG. 9	SEPT. 23	NOV. 7	DEC. 22	FEB. 5
60° North	89°	55°	37°	55°	89°	122°	140°	122°
30° North	90°	71°	63°	71°	90°	108°	116°	108°
0° (Equator)	90°	74°	67°	74°	90°	106°	113°	106°
30° South	90°	72°	64°	72°	90°	104°	117°	109°

134. Geographic north and south may be found by the shadow cast by the sun. If you have the correct local time on your watch, the shadow cast by an object at 1200 hours will indicate north and south. The object must be straight and perpendicular to the ground. In the northern hemisphere the base of the shadow will indicate south and the tip of the shadow will indicate north. If you have no watch you may still obtain direction by the shadow cast by the sun. Place a stick or other straight object in the ground on a level spot. Starting in the morning and continuing throughout the day, about once every hour, mark the point at the tip of the shadow. At the end connect these points and you will have a line running true east and west. A perpendicular to this line will indicate north and south.

135. By night, if the sky is clear, true north and south can be determined by the stars. In the northern hemisphere, true north can be ascertained from the constellation of the Great Bear, which points to Polaris (North Star). In the southern hemisphere, the Southern Cross indicates true south.

136. Once course has been set, direction should be maintained by compass. If you have no compass, pick two easily visible objects which are exactly on the line you want to follow and as far apart as possible, and keep them in line while walking. Before reaching the first object, pick a third landmark in the same line ahead and repeat the process. This method is not always reliable or feasible in featureless country, such as that encountered in most deserts.

137. When resting, face in the direction of travel or make a pointer on the ground so that when you resume the march you are certain of travelling in the same direction.

How to Determine Distance

138. Distances in the desert can be deceptive. Owing to the clear atmosphere, objects appear to be much closer than they actually are. Visual estimations of distance should be multiplied by three. To keep an accurate check of distance travelled, and to be able to plot this on your map, it is necessary to evolve a more accurate method of determining distance than just by visual estimations.

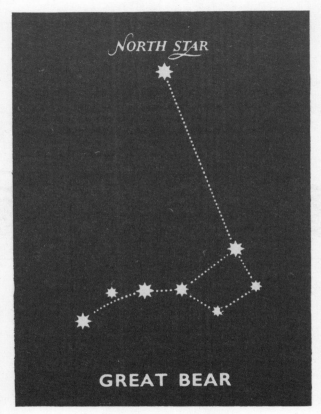

NORTH STAR

GREAT BEAR

GREAT BEAR AND NORTH STAR

43

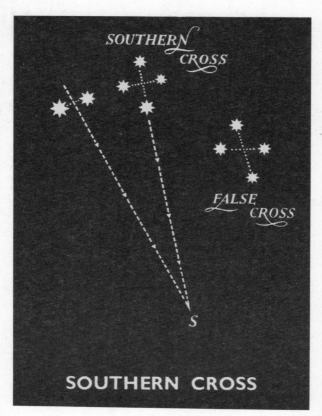

SOUTHERN CROSS

139. On level, open ground with a good surface, the average individual walks about 2½ miles per hour. With practice, a good estimation of the distance travelled can be made by reference to your watch. Another method that is even more accurate, and probably safer to use in desert travel, is to count the number of paces taken. The natural stride of a man is about 2½ feet (10 feet every 4 steps). A combination of both methods can be used to check the accuracy of one against the other.

How to Plot Direction and Distance

140. A protractor and scale are necessary to plot direction and distance.

141. If a protractor is not available, one can be improvised from a piece of paper as shown in the accompanying diagram. Fold the paper as illustrated. When it is unfolded, the angles formed by the creases should be marked in pencil.

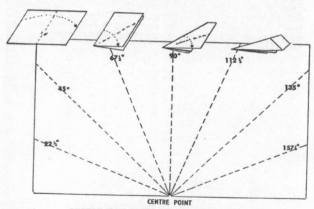

CENTRE POINT

PROTRACTOR MADE BY FOLDING PAPER

45

142. A scale can also be improvised by folding a strip of paper into equal divisions. Mark the creases at the edge of the paper and let each division represent 1,000 feet, or any other convenient interval you choose to plot.

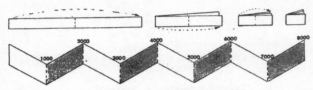

SCALE IMPROVISED FROM FOLDED PAPER

143. If an obstacle should force you to alter the direction of travel, the alteration of course should be determined by compass and the distance by pace counting. This will enable the alteration to be plotted and the new direction and distance estimated to reach the objective or to resume the original line of travel.

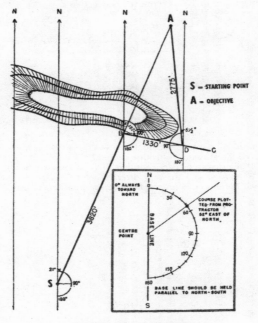

HOW TO PLOT A COURSE

47

Ground/Air Emergency Code for Use In Air/Land Rescue Search

KEY

1 REQUIRE DOCTOR, SERIOUS INJURIES
2 REQUIRE MEDICAL SUPPLIES
3 UNABLE TO PROCEED
4 REQUIRE FOOD AND WATER
5 REQUIRE FIREARMS AND AMMUNITION
6 REQUIRE MAP AND COMPASS
7 REQUIRE SIGNAL LAMP WITH BATTERY, & RADIO
8 INDICATE DIRECTION TO PROCEED
9 AM PROCEEDING IN THIS DIRECTION
10 WILL ATTEMPT TAKE-OFF
11 AIRCRAFT SERIOUSLY DAMAGED
12 PROBABLY SAFE TO LAND HERE
13 REQUIRE FUEL AND OIL
14 ALL WELL
15 NO
16 YES
17 NOT UNDERSTOOD
18 REQUIRE ENGINEER

CODE

* A SPACE OF 10FT BETWEEN ELEMENTS WHEREVER POSSIBLE

ARCTIC

SURVIVAL

AIR MINISTRY PAMPHLET 226

ARCTIC SURVIVAL

INTRODUCTION

1. Survival depends on two, largely psychological, factors: the determination to live and the elimination of fear. Fear is caused through ignorance, in other words *inadequate training*. However, no amount of training or other material aid will suffice without the natural instinct of self-preservation.

2. **The Arctic.** The Arctic has been defined geographically as the area north of the Arctic Circle at latitude 66°33′N. From the survival aspect, however, it is more practical to consider the area north of the timber line as Arctic. Along certain Siberian rivers forests grow up to 400 miles north of the Arctic Circle, while along the west shore of the Hudson Bay the tree line is 400 miles south of the Circle. These areas north of the timber line, with a mean annual temperature below 32°F., are known as "barren lands". The region includes the north coasts of Alaska, Canada, Scandinavia, and the U.S.S.R.; the Canadian Arctic Archipelago, Greenland, and the majority of Iceland.

3. **The Sub-Arctic.** The sub-arctic is a belt of coniferous vegetation of variable width south of the Arctic Circle. Within it the mean annual temperature is above 32°F. It includes most of Alaska and the interior of Canada, the northern territories of the U.S.S.R., and most of Scandinavia. The term must be used flexibly.

4. **Other Cold Regions.** The principles of arctic survival have to be applied to other mountainous or desolate regions where low temperatures at high altitudes, high winds, a permanent snow covering, or other wintry phenomena prevail at various times. These regions include the Rocky Mountains, the Andes, and the Himalayas.

5. **The Arctic Climate.** The Arctic is bleak, and in the winter cold, but it is not, as many people think, a region of continual snowstorms and howling gales where the temperature is always "sixty below". Many Eskimos and quite a few white people live

there contentedly. The idea that snow is always falling arises from the fact that snow is easily stirred by the wind long after it has stopped falling. The two seasons, a long winter and a short summer, are clearly defined and the temperature varies considerably. In general, the interior areas have the coldest winters and the warmest summers. A temperature of —96°F. has been recorded in Central Siberia. At the other end of the scale, temperatures of 80°F. in the shade are common in many places north of the Arctic Circle. The annual temperature range may be as much as 176°F.; as at Fort Yukon, on the Arctic Circle, where a maximum summer temperature of 100°F. in the shade, and a minimum winter temperature of —76°F., have been recorded. With these high temperatures it is not unusual to find a summer landscape which can be favourably compared with the Orkneys and Shetlands.

PRE-FLIGHT PREPARATION

Prepare for Trouble

6. The best time to start learning what to do when you have been forced down in arctic regions is before the event. The correct preparation involves acquiring a thorough knowledge of:—

    (a) Cold-weather flying clothing.

    (b) Safety and survival equipment.

    (c) Emergency drills and procedures.

    (d) The principles of survival.

Cold-Weather Flying Clothing

7. Cold-weather flying clothing has been designed to enable aircrew to fly effectively in any types of aircraft, and particular emphasis has been made on freedom of movement. The main essentials are to keep windproof outer materials intact over sufficient inner insulative clothing, and the avoidance of any tight or restrictive clothing. In survival conditions you must depend for warmth, not on fires or fuel stoves, but on your clothing. Your clothing is your first line of defence against low temperatures and high winds. BE PREPARED. Dress for the possible emergency and adjust the temperature of the cockpit accordingly.

8. Inner Clothing. The principle of correct underclothing is not thickness but insulation. Air in fact forms the main insulation of all materials used in clothing. The inner flying clothing consists of multiple layers of loosely fitting garments each designed to fit over the clothing immediately beneath it, holding a layer of air between the garments. Your inner clothing will normally consist of:—

(a) A string vest made of thick cotton cord, knitted in a wide mesh. The wide mesh holds a layer of air in contact with the body.

Fig. I.
Cold Weather Flying Clothing

(b) Pyjama-type inner trousers worn under war service or flying dress trousers. The looseness of the underpants holds air and allows free circulation and ventilation. In very cold conditions two pairs should be worn.

(c) A woollen aircrew shirt with attached collar and buttoning cuffs. A tie should not be worn during flight because it would restrict ventilation at the neck.

(d) A long-sleeved, slit-necked, ribbed woollen pollover. A draw cord is provided at the neck opening to help in the control of ventilation.

(e) A necksquare made of soft cotton and resembling a large dishcloth. It effectively protects the neck opening and allows some ventilation at the neck. It is designed to protect the face in high wind conditions, and at night when the face is the only part of the body not protected by the sleeping bag.

9. **Outer Clothing.** Outer garments must be windproof and durable. The weave must be close to prevent snow compacting into the material. A certain degree of porosity is necessary to allow water vapour to escape and evaporate in the cold dry air. You will normally wear:—

(a) A cold-weather flying overall which is essentially two garments, trousers and jacket, which have been combined to make an overall as this is more effective in flight conditions. For ground survival the jacket, or inner parka, and the trousers can be separated to allow adequate ventilation. Draw cords are provided at the bottoms of the trousers legs: these are intended for use in survival conditions to help in keeping snow out of the trousers and boot tops. A hood is attached to the jacket and in normal flying conditions it is folded neatly at the back. The face aperture can be closed by a draw cord.

(b) A cold-weather cap made of windproof material and lined with woollen fabric. It may be worn alone or under the hood of the flying overall or outer parka. The cap has internally stowed flaps which can be turned down to give protection to the back of the neck, ears, and forehead.

(c) An outer parka to be worn in extreme cold over the flying overall. It has both windproof and insulating properties. The collar, to which the hood is attached, is fur-lined. The hood, closed by a draw cord, is designed to protect the face in high wind chill conditions. An extension to the hood, for use in the severest weather, consists of an adjustable wire-stiffened curtain edged with wolverine fur, and helps in preventing the wind reaching the face.

10. **Handwear.** Handwear must be insulating and windproof, and must not be tight. Mittens are preferred to gloves as the fingers will give mutual warmth, but mittens are not ideal for aircrew. The handwear assembly consists of:—

(a) Long woollen wristlets which give protection to the wrist and the back of the hand.

(b) Inner mitts made of wool.

(*c*) Outer mitts made of soft leather. The palm of the hand is lined with a wool pile material, and a pad of the same material is sewn on the back. This pad is used for warming the nose or the face in the event of frostbite, and also as a nose wiper.

(*d*) Working gloves, made with leather fronts and fabric backs, to be worn over the wristlets.

11. **Footwear.**

(*a*) *The Mukluk Assembly* is worn instead of flying boots by aircrew operating in dry cold conditions. It consists of:—

    (i) Three pairs of woollen socks sized to fit over one another without creasing.

    (ii) A duffle sock made of blanketing and sized to fit effectively over the woollen socks.

    (iii) A thick felt insole, with a ventilating mesh sole, worn downwards, to provide effective insulation beneath the foot.

    (iv) A mukluk which has a waterproof canvas upper extending over the calf and a rubber sole and galosh. The sole is ribbed for good traction on snow. The top of the boot can be closed by a draw cord.

(*b*) *The Boucheron* is worn by personnel operating in wet cold conditions. This boot has a leather waterproof upper extending to just below the knee, and a rubber sole and galosh. It is unlined but has a removable felt insole. It may be worn over the woollen socks and duffle sock as required.

Safety and Survival Equipment

12. Before each flight carefully check all aircraft emergency packs and your personal survival kit and safety equipment. Equipment on personal loan should be inspected daily. Ensure that all the articles in your personal survival pack are serviceable and that none is missing. Resist the temptation to "borrow" desirable items for your personal use. Make yourself thoroughly familiar with the operation of your safety equipment. Do not misuse it; rough handling may lead to failure at a critical time. Since weight and bulk are the limiting factors in the amount of survival equipment that can be carried in an aircraft, your parachute,

lifejacket, and dinghy, are regarded as supplementary survival equipment. Study your safety equipment from this angle; look upon your parachute as potential shelter, clothing, or fishing equipment. Likewise, each item in your survival packs has been selected and designed to have as many uses as possible. Learn them all NOW.

Emergency Drills and Procedures

13. It is not within the scope of this pamphlet to discuss emergency drills and procedures in detail. A.M. Pamphlet 212, "Emergencies", and the Command Emergency Drills deal fully with these subjects. Emergency drills should be practised regularly, so that the drill will be almost automatic even in total darkness, and you should thoroughly know the emergency signals procedure and the rescue facilities available in the area over which you intend to fly.

Principles of Survival

14. If you wish to survive an emergency descent into the Arctic, there are certain things you must do. This pamphlet tells you what to do and in many cases how to do it. A copy of the pamphlet will be inside your survival pack. Read it for the first time in the comfort of a crew-room, not on an ice floe drifting in the Arctic Sea.

ACTION IN AN EMERGENCY

Communication

15. The provision of effective help to aircraft and personnel in distress depends, to a large extent, on the receipt of timely and accurate information by the ground organization. When the captain of an aircraft considers that a state of "Safety", "Urgency", or "Distress", exists, the appropriate signals should be transmitted in accordance with the current procedures. Do not hesitate to let the world and your crew know that an emergency exists.

Abandon Aircraft or Crash-land?

16. If an emergency arises over the Arctic, land the aircraft if it is at all possible. Abandon the aircraft only if the terrain is

extremely hazardous or in the event of structural failure or fire in the air. Landing with the aircraft has the advantages of providing a readily distinguishable marker for search aircraft, and many parts of the aircraft will prove invaluable later on.

Abandoning Aircraft

17. If you do have to abandon the aircraft take as much equipment as possible with you. If you have followed the practice of wearing all your cold-weather flying clothing you will leave the aircraft with adequate protection against the cold. Note the position of the crashed aircraft; even a burnt-out wreck may be of some use. Large crews should decide, before the emergency arises, on a method of assembly after abandoning aircraft. Here are two suggested procedures:—

(a) Bail-out on a straight course. The crew can assemble progressively. The two end men, the first and last out, move inward toward the middle men, linking up with others on the way. The magnetic track of the aircraft should be given to all the crew before they bail-out. The middle man should light a fire and make smoke signals, and flash his heliograph to mark the rendezvous.

(b) Bail-out in a circle and all personnel converge toward the centre.

In both procedures the crew should bail-out in quick succession to ensure that they will not be too widely dispersed.

Crash Landing

18. When searching for a place to land, stay on track if it is at all possible. Do not wander aimlessly until all the fuel has gone; endeavour to make a crash landing under power. Successful forced landings have been made on frozen lakes or rivers, beaches, large ice floes, glaciers or ice-caps, and treeless valleys. Always land with your wheels UP.

19. If there is a choice do not land on frozen lakes or rivers during the thaw or freeze-up; the ice may be too thin. Do not land on sea ice which appears dark in colour, or on any ice free from snow drifts. You should normally land into wind: blowing snow will give you an indication of the wind direction. However, the

presence of pressure ridges, formed when ice floes grind into or ride up over each other, and tightly packed snow drifts, will necessitate a landing parallel to the ridges or drifts.

IMMEDIATE ACTIONS AFTER A CRASH LANDING

20. Get out of the aircraft as quickly as possible, taking with you your safety and survival equipment. Be cautious as to the state of the ground around the aircraft. Deep crevasses may exist in glaciated regions and avalanches may be prevalent on steep slopes. Stay away from the aircraft until the danger of fire has passed and then remove all useful items of equipment from the aircraft. The battery should be removed and kept as warm as possible. It is advisable to spread a parachute on the snow and place all the equipment on it to prevent loss. First aid for the injured is the next consideration. While first aid is being given, make certain that everyone is properly dressed. Special clothing, such as anti-G suits, which tend to restrict circulation, should be loosened or taken off.

21. **First Aid.** Check all the crew for injuries and shock. All injured personnel should be kept as warm as possible to prevent frostbite or freezing. Follow the established practices:—

(a) *Wounds.* See that open wounds are dressed to prevent infection; do not handle the wound and keep the wounded part at rest. Clothing should be cut away with care. Slit it carefully so that it can be sewn up again after the wound has been treated.

(b) *Fractures.* Fractured limbs should be immobilized by splints. Do not use metal parts of the aircraft for splints. Do not remove clothing from the limb, but cut it away from wounds and dress them before splinting.

(c) *Haemorrhage.* Bleeding will normally be stopped by the blood congealing in the very low temperature. If necessary apply a tourniquet between the injury and the heart, at the pressure point nearest to the injury. Release the tourniquet for a half-a-minute every fifteen to twenty minutes, and remove it entirely as soon as possible.

(d) **Shock and Internal Injury.** Keep the injured person lying down and warm. If he is conscious a hot drink can be given, provided the injury is not abdominal.

(e) **Burns.** Don't open blisters. Use the anti-burn cream in the first-aid kit. Don't change the bandage and keep the burned part at rest.

(f) **Cessation of Breathing.** If an injured man has stopped breathing, pull his tongue forward and apply artificial respiration. Check for head injuries or fractured skull, indicated by unequal pupils or bleeding from the ears or into the skin around the eyes.

22. **Drain the Oil.** If possible, oil should be drained from the engine sump and oil tank to provide an immediate source of fuel for heat and cooking. Failure to do so as soon as possible will result in the oil becoming congealed and impossible to drain. A receptacle is not vital, as the oil can be drained on to the ground where it will congeal quickly.

23. **Sundry Hints.** When the immediate tasks have been completed start a fire in a sheltered spot and sit down and relax. Firm handling of the situation is necessary from the start. The captain of the aircraft will assume command of the party, but if another member of the crew is better qualified he should always be consulted before any major decisions are made. The provision of shelter, warmth, and food, and the preparation of the emergency signalling equipment should be attended to next. Detail the crew members for camp duties according to their capabilities and fitness; but do not overwork the willing horse. For duties away from the immediate camp site men should work in pairs, so that they can watch each other's faces for the first signs of frostbite. Injured members of the party should be given small tasks to do, to occupy their minds and to overcome the feeling that they are a burden on the survivors. Such duties could include whittling wood for kindling, making fish nets, and log keeping. The log should tell the complete story from the beginning of the emergency to your safe return to civilization. All observations, however trivial they may seem at the time, should be recorded.

EMERGENCY SIGNALS

24. As soon as possible all your emergency signalling equipment should be prepared for use. Search aircraft have often flown

over or near the scene of a crash without seeing it. Survivors should take turns keeping watch for search aircraft and everyone should be familiar with the location and operation of the emergency signalling equipment. One of the best ground signals is the aircraft itself; and to achieve the maximum contrast against a background of snow, its surfaces should be kept clear of snow and frost. If your dinghy and weather apron are not required for anything more important, use them to make signal strips and compose a message from the Ground/Air Emergency Code. Make the kite of the "Gibson Girl" more conspicuous by attaching a long tail to it. The tail can be made from a parachute canopy and coloured with fluorescene sea marker. Make the camp site as conspicuous as possible from the air.

Fig. 2. Display of Ground Signals

Radio Signals

25. Aircraft W/T. The aircraft W/T is your best means of communication. If transmissions are made, the message, bearing an S.O.S. priority, should include the aircraft callsign, the estimated position, a 20-second dash, and the time at which you intend to transmit again. Transmissions on 500 Kcs. should start at 15 and 45 minutes past each hour, for periods of three minutes. In the low winter temperatures the batteries will be very weak, and transmissions should be made as soon as possible after the crash before the batteries freeze.

26. The Standard Dinghy Radio Kit—SCR 578— "Gibson Girl".

(*a*) The transmitter should be operated for periods of four minutes, at intervals of about ten minutes. But if a serviceable and accurate watch is available, you should transmit for periods of three minutes starting at 15 and 45 minutes past each hour.

(*b*) With the signals set to automatic, the signals take the following form:—

(i) Auto 1 Position—S.O.S. for 20 seconds followed by a continuous dash for 20 seconds.

(ii) Auto 2 Position—S.O.S. for 20 seconds followed by four-second dashes for 20 seconds.

As the Auto 2 Position is designed to operate the automatic alarm on surface vessels, transmissions in Arctic regions should be confined to the Auto 1 Position, unless it is estimated that the crash position is such that transmissions on the Auto 2 Position may be received by surface craft. In this case the four-minute period should consist of two minutes on the Auto 1 Position followed by two minutes on the Auto 2 Position.

(*c*) If the crash position is known, this can be transmitted along with any other information, on the Manual Position, outside the above periods.

(*d*) For convenience the transmitter may be strapped to a tree. If the wind is not strong enough to fly the kite, you may extend the aerial to its maximum length between trees: to earth the set, extend the spare reel of aerial wire parallel to and below the aerial and fasten the "ground" lead to this.

If there are no trees, extend the aerial to its maximum length along the ground: to earth the set, extend the spare reel of aerial wire along the surface of the ground in the opposite direction to the aerial, and fasten it to the "ground" lead.

27. **Transmitter T3180—"Walter".** With a maximum range of 20 to 25 miles, "Walter" should be used only when it is estimated that search aircraft are in the vicinity. It is pointless to switch on "Walter" immediately after the crash, unless the aircraft is on a recognized route frequented by other aircraft. The transmitter should be switched on for periods of two minutes at five-minute intervals, and should be left switched on if aircraft are seen or heard. In Arctic conditions the battery should be worn permanently under one's clothing and attached to the transmitter by a wandering lead.

Shadow Signals

28. One of the best shadow signals in winter is snow writing. Trenches cut in the snow to form a message are easy to make. They can be made simply by scuffling up snow as one walks along. The bigger the size of the letter and the deeper the shadow, the more effective is the signal. Normally, however, 30-foot letters are big enough. Shadows may be deepened by cutting the trenches and piling the snow where it will throw the longest shadow along the letters; that is, write your message facing north or south and pile the snow to the south of the letters. The writing or the geometrical design can be brought into sharper contrast with the snow by filling the trench with spruce boughs or parts of the aircraft, or by mixing the fluorescent sea marker with water and sprinkling it in the trench. In summer, writing can be made in the sand. On the tundra, sod blocks can be cut out and set aside to cast shadows on the bare earth. Logs or rocks can be laid out on any surface. In spring, snow drifts can often be found in willows, under high banks and in gullies, long after snow has gone from the flat country. It can be shovelled on to dark ground to form signals. When snow lays lightly on the tundra, dig down to expose the dark contrasting tundra. In the deep Arctic winter, a full or almost full moon will throw excellent shadows of well-prepared trench writing on snow surfaces. The best signals are either S.O.S. or ⊕. Qualifying signals should be taken from the Ground/Air Emergency Code. (Fig. 3.)

Ground/Air Emergency Code for Use In Air/Land Rescue Search

KEY

1 REQUIRE DOCTOR, SERIOUS INJURIES
2 REQUIRE MEDICAL SUPPLIES
3 UNABLE TO PROCEED
4 REQUIRE FOOD AND WATER
5 REQUIRE FIREARMS AND AMMUNITION
6 REQUIRE MAP AND COMPASS
7 REQUIRE SIGNAL LAMP WITH BATTERY, & RADIO
8 INDICATE DIRECTION TO PROCEED
9 AM PROCEEDING IN THIS DIRECTION

10 WILL ATTEMPT TAKE-OFF
11 AIRCRAFT SERIOUSLY DAMAGED
12 PROBABLY SAFE TO LAND HERE
13 REQUIRE FUEL AND OIL
14 ALL WELL
15 NO
16 YES
17 NOT UNDERSTOOD
18 REQUIRE ENGINEER

CODE

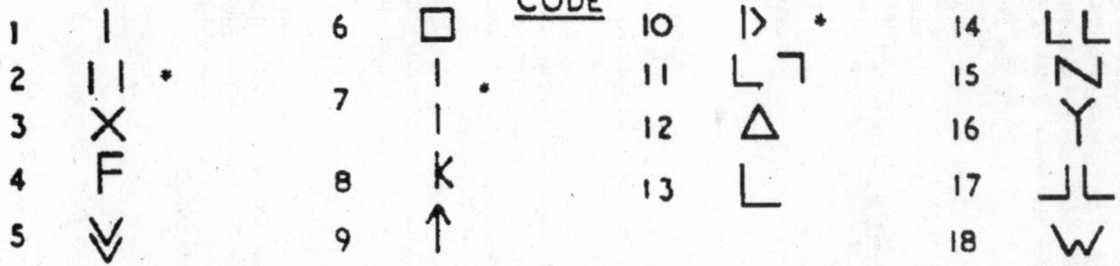

* A SPACE OF 10FT BETWEEN ELEMENTS WHEREVER POSSIBLE

Fig. 3.

Fire and Smoke Signals

29. Smoke signals are satisfactory only on calm clear days. Winds and blowing snow tend to disperse the smoke, so that it is visible only at very short distances. Create a smoke which will be in contrast to the background; *i.e.* white smoke in summer and black in winter. White smoke can be made by throwing green grass and boughs on the fires, and black smoke by throwing on rubber or oil.

30. Signal fires should not be burned continuously if fuel is scarce. The fires should be prepared and covered to prevent the materials from getting wet or covered with snow. Three signal fires arranged in a triangle is a distress sign. If convenient, use the camp fire as one of the signal fires. Otherwise arrange the fires around the camp site, so that they can be reached and lit with a minimum of delay.

31. The spruce torch (*i.e.* a flaming spruce tree) is an excellent signal by day or night. Select a tree with very dense foliage, and shake off as much snow and ice as possible from the upper branches. If all the trees in the vicinity are sparse, break branches from other trees, shake them free of snow and weave them in the upper branches of the selected tree. Then collect kindling and build a "bird's nest" in the lower branches to act as the ignitor. If possible have a can of fuel or oil at hand to hasten the ignition. Cover the "bird's nest" for protection against the weather, and so that newly accumulated snow can be knocked off the tree without falling on to the kindling. The "bird's nest" will ignite the spruce tips until the whole tree is ablaze and visible for miles.

Light Signals

32. Use the heliograph for signalling if the sun is shining. Heliographs can be improvised from any polished surfaces, such as cowlings and ration tins. Signalling by these means should be practised regularly so that there is no delay in focusing when an aircraft is sighted.

33. At night your best light signals are the torch and the flash fire. The flash fire is made by soaking a large piece of fabric in high octane fuel, spreading it out on the ground and lighting it.

When using a signalling torch or the signalling lamp of the "Gibson Girl", do not point it in the direction of the search aircraft. Illuminate a reflective surface, such as an inverted cowling or any snow-covered surfaces, by pointing the beam downwards at a low angle so that a large lighted circle is reflected. Keep the light moving or flash S.O.S. to improve the chances of being seen.

Pyrotechnics

34. You will have a limited supply of emergency pyrotechnics, and possibly the aircraft signal pistol and cartridges. Fire them only when you are fairly certain that there is a chance of them being seen by the search aircraft. The search aircraft at night, using the Night Search Technique, will fire green cartridges every 5 to 10 minutes. When the survivors see a green light, they should wait for the aircraft to clear the glare and then fire a red pyrotechnic; after a short interval fire a second one. If the search aircraft sees the reds he will turn towards the first one and check his course on the second one, at the same time firing a succession of green lights until he is overhead. The survivors should conserve their pyrotechnics, and only fire a third red signal when the aircraft is almost overhead or is going off course.

SHELTER

35. In the winter you cannot stay in the open and expect to live, unless you are on the move. You must have shelter even if it is only a hole in the snow. Shelter is less important in summer, but it will provide comfort and relaxation under the most ideal conditions. The type of shelter you elect to build will depend on:—

(a) What tools are available.

(b) What materials are available.

(c) What you need shelter from—wind, snow, cold, rain, or insects.

(d) How long you expect to remain in that location.

Regardless of the type, the shelter must provide adequate ventilation to prevent carbon monoxide poisoning and to allow moisture to escape.

Selection of Site

36. A summer camp site should not be on low-lying ground, which is likely to be damp, or on areas that might be flooded. Select a spot in a cool breeze to keep the insects away, either on top of a ridge, or the shores of a cold lake, or a place that gets an onshore breeze. The lee of boulders and shelving rocks should provide dry camp sites.

37. During winter, protection from the wind is a prime consideration. Avoid the lee of slopes and cliffs where snow may drift heavily and bury your shelter.

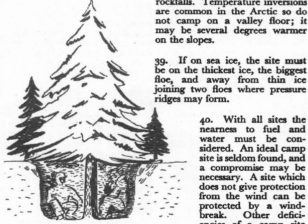

38. In mountain camp sites avoid areas which you suspect are subject to avalanches, floods, and rockfalls. Temperature inversions are common in the Arctic so do not camp on a valley floor; it may be several degrees warmer on the slopes.

39. If on sea ice, the site must be on the thickest ice, the biggest floe, and away from thin ice joining two floes where pressure ridges may form.

40. With all sites the nearness to fuel and water must be considered. An ideal camp site is seldom found, and a compromise may be necessary. A site which does not give protection from the wind can be protected by a wind-break. Other deficiencies of a camp site may be similarly overcome.

Fig. 4. Natural Hole under a Tree converted into a Shelter

Natural Shelters

41. Caves and overhanging rockshelves will often provide dry shelters. They should be used in the winter only if well insulated, and in summer only if they can be made insect-proof. In timbered country where the snow is deep, spruce trees often provide ready-made shelters. The natural hole under the lower branches will provide a quickly available shelter. The lower branches at snow level will form the roof. (Fig. 4.)

Aeroplane Shelters

42. In the summer the fuselage will make an adequate shelter if it is on safe ground; it is waterproof and can be made insect-proof with parachutes. It SHOULD NOT be used as a shelter in winter unless it is well insulated. The metal is a good conductor of heat and will quickly dissipate any available heat. In winter you can make two types of shelters using a wing or tailplane as a roof or support. The first, a snow block shelter, is made by piling up snow blocks to form a windbreak, walled shelter, or snow-house. The second is made by hanging engine covers or a parachute over the wing. The loose ends can be anchored by rocks or piles of snow.

Fig. 5. Wing-Snowblock Shelter

Parachute Shelters

43. **Paratepee.** An excellent shelter for protection against drizzly weather and insects is made from a parachute canopy. In it you can build a fire, cook, eat, sleep, dress, and make signals— all without going out of doors. You will need ten good poles about 12 to 14 feet long, and half a parachute canopy. The method of construction is shown in the illustrations. The other half of the canopy can be used as additional tenting to provide insulation, should the weather demand it.

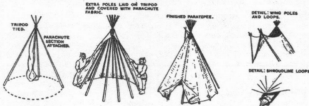

Fig. 6.   Construction of Paratepee

44. **Pup Tent.** A simple pup tent can be made by placing a rope or pole between two trees or stakes and draping a parachute over it. Stretch the corners down and secure them with stones or pegs.

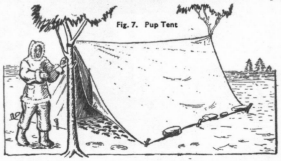

Fig. 7.   Pup Tent

45. Simple Bell Tents. A constructed. Always use the provide adequate insulation.
variety of bell tents can be double layer principle to

Fig. 8. Simple Parachute Shelter

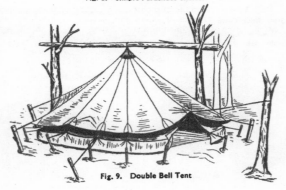

Fig. 9. Double Bell Tent

46. Willow Shelter. Where willows are plentiful this shelter can be made very quickly. The floor area should just accommodate the sleeping bags and the maximum height should just allow the occupants to sit up without their heads touching the roof. The tunnel-like construction is shown in Fig. 10. The framework can be covered with several layers of parachute canopy, which may be anchored with snow.

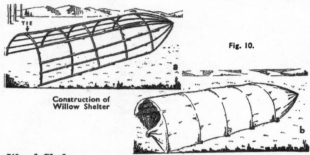

Fig. 10.

Construction of
Willow Shelter

Wood Shelters

47. Lean-to and Bough Shelters. If you are in timbered country and have plenty of wood, the best shelter is a lean-to.

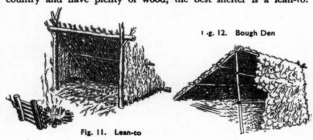

Fig. 12. Bough Den

Fig. 11. Lean-to

A good three-man lean-to is shown in Fig. 11. The roof can be covered by sod blocks, spruce boughs, or any suitable material salvaged from the aircraft. Spruce tips and similar materials should be woven in from the top like a tiled roof to prevent rain from entering the shelter. A quickly improvized temporary shelter is a two-sided bough den (Fig. 12); it requires fewer poles and less time to build than a lean-to, but it cannot be water-proofed as efficiently.

Snow Shelters

48. The type of snow shelter you can construct will depend on the quality of the snow. You will have to decide whether or not the snow is suitable for cutting up into snow blocks. The ideal snow for snow block shelters is that upon which a man can walk without breaking through or leaving deeply embedded footprints. The snow must also be tested by pressing a probe into it slowly; if it goes in evenly the snow is ideal for cutting snow blocks. Snow blocks should measure about 18 inches wide by 30 inches long and four to eight inches thick. Blocks of this size should be easy to cut and handle. They will be thick enough to provide good insulation and strength, yet thin enough to allow maximum penetration of the sun's rays. The lighter the interior the warmer it will be and fuel will not have to be used for light. In addition, a light inside a snow block shelter makes a good beacon at night.

49. **Snow Trench.** The ideal snow block shelter is the snow trench, which is designed for one man. Start the construction by marking out a rectangular floor area; big enough to accommodate only one sleeping bag. Remove the snow from this area, by cutting out snow blocks, to the full width of the trench and to a depth of four feet. Along the top edges of the sides of the trench, cut an L-shaped step six inches deep and six inches wide; these steps serve as a base for the snow blocks when the trench is roofed. At the end away from the entrance, place two blocks on the steps on each side of the trench and lean them together to start forming an inverted V roof. The two blocks should be offset, so that after the first pair of blocks are joined, it will be necessary to handle only one block at a time. Each end of the roof should be covered

with blocks and an entrance dug through the snow at the downwind end. If the snow is not four feet deep, the walls can be constructed of snow blocks to the required height.

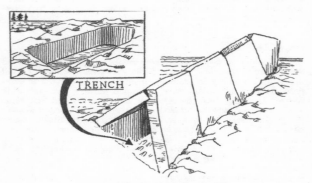

Fig. 13. Construction of Snow Trench

50. Snow Caves and Snow Holes.

(a) A snow cave can be dug wherever snowdrifts of sufficient depth can be found. Caves are difficult to dig without getting wet and are therefore less desirable than a trench-type shelter. The roof of the cave should be arched to allow moisture to run down the walls without dripping. Also, an arched ceiling will not sag readily from the weight of the snow above.

(b) An excellent temporary shelter can be constructed by simply digging a hole in the snow and using your parachute canopy as a roof.

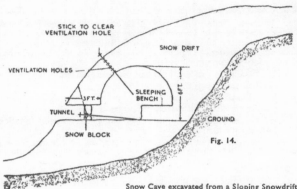

Fig. 14.

Snow Cave excavated from a Sloping Snowdrift

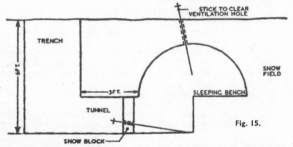

Fig. 15.

Snow Cave dug from the Side of a Trench in a Flat Snowfield

51. **Big crews should build individual or two-man snow shelters radiating from a central or communal entrance. The entrance can be protected by a circular snow wall and tented with a parachute canopy.**

Beds and Bedding

52. In snow shelters beds should be made on a sleeping bench which will raise you into the warmer air of the shelter. In all types of shelters beds should be well insulated from the actual floor of the shelter. Depending on your resources the following make good insulating material:—

(a) Parachute canopy, backpad, or seat cushion.

(b) Inverted dinghy.

(c) Lifejacket.

(d) Seat cushions, asbestos, etc., from the aircraft.

(e) Ferns, shrubs, lichens, moss, evergreen boughs (particularly spruce tips).

Your insulating can be as thick as time permits; six inches at least is desirable. Rearrange it regularly to prevent it packing down.

Practical Hints

53. The following points should not be neglected:—

(a) The smaller the shelter the warmer it will be.

(b) Adequate ventilation to prevent asphyxiation and carbon monoxide poisoning is of vital importance.

(c) Two ventilation holes, one near the top of the shelter and the other at the entrance, must be kept clear. One ventilation hole is not sufficient, as the air cannot then circulate

(d) Shovels and tools must be taken into snow shelters, as it may often be necessary to dig a way out if snowfalls or drifting occur.

(e) The entrance of each shelter must be clearly marked so that it can easily be found.

(f) A mark should be made on the snow above each shelter to show its position and to prevent men from walking over the roof.

(g) Drips in snow shelters can be stopped by putting a piece of snow on the source of the drip.

(h) The roof should be at least twelve inches thick unless the snow is very hard, when six inches may be sufficient.

(j) Snow floors should be well tramped down before starting to build the shelter.

54. During survival you are kept warm by a combination of body heat, insulative clothing, and shelter. However, you will need a fire to prepare hot food and drinks in order to maintain and replenish your body heat. A fire is also necessary for drying clothes, for signalling, and to provide external heat. In extreme cold, however, very little heat can be obtained from a fire unless you get so close that you are liable to scorch your clothing. A fire will increase your morale, particularly during the long dark winter days.

55. Your immediate source of heat for cooking is supplied by the emergency stove in the aircraft survival pack; however, this will not be available should you bale out. Your personal survival pack contains candles, which are most suitable for heating snow shelters, fire-making tablets, and matches. These immediate sources of heat may be supplemented, according to your natural fuel supply, by open fires and improvized stoves.

Fires

56. The main ingredients for a good open fire are a good fireplace, kindling, fuel, and a means of lighting the kindling. To these can be added a little knowledge and a lot of patience.

Fig. 16. Log Platform for Fire

Fig. 17. Log Reflector for Fire

57. Fireplaces. Prepare the location of your fires carefully. Don't build a fire under a snow-covered tree—snow may fall and put out the fire. Protect domestic fires from the wind, and so save fuel. Build the fires on a firm platform; use green logs, stones, cowlings, or dig down to firm soil. Cooking fires should be walled in by green logs or stones, not only to concentrate the heat but to provide a platform for your cooking pot. Fires for warming shelters should be built against a reflector of rocks or green logs to direct the heat into the shelter.

Fig. 18. Cooking Platform

58. Kindling. You will need some easily inflammable kindling to get a fire going. Pick up kindling whenever you can find it, even if you do not expect to make camp for some hours. Gather birch bark, dry lichens, twigs, resinous shrubs, bits of fat (if not required for food), feathers, tufts of dry grass and sedges, against the possibility of a shortage of good kindling at the camp site. Larger twigs can be cut in "feather fashion" if kindling is scarce.

Fig. 19. Birch Bark Under-layers   Fig. 20. Feathering Wood for Tinder

Paper or rags and twigs soaked in fuel or oil are good **artificial** kindling.

59. **Natural Fuel.**

(*a*) *Wood.* Even in polar regions there are clumps of dwarf willow and birch. Birch is oily and if split fine will burn even if wet. Standing deadwood and dead branches provide your best fuel; the dead trees can be easily pushed over and chopped up. Lying deadwood and driftwood is likely to be frozen or waterlogged and is useless unless dried out. Green timber can be burned on a hot fire.

(*b*) *Coal.* Outcrops may be found occasionally on the surface and coal may be found washed up on beaches.

(*c*) *Animal Fats.* Use animal fats for food rather than fuel. You will derive more heat from fat you eat than from fat you burn.

(*d*) *Gassiope.* In some barren grounds, where there is no driftwood and little willow or birch, the Eskimos depend almost entirely on this plant for fuel. It is a low, spreading, evergreen plant, with tiny leaves and white bell-shaped flowers. It grows from four to twelve inches high and contains so much resin that it will burn even when green or wet.

(*e*) In treeless areas you can find other natural fuels such as dry grass which can be twisted into bunches, peat dry enough to burn (found at the top of undercut river banks), and dried animal dung. Try anything for fuel, but in small quantities until you are certain of its qualities.

Firelighting

60. Get all your materials together before you try to start the fire. Make sure your kindling and fuel are dry, and have enough fuel on hand to keep the fire going. Arrange a small amount of kindling in a low pyramid, close enough together to allow the flames to lick from one piece to another. Leave a small opening for lighting. Save matches by using a candle to light the fire, or make a faggot of thin dry twigs tied loosely. Apply the lighted candle or faggot to the lower windward side of the kindling, shielding it from the wind as you do so. Use the firemaking tablets only

Light your fire with a candle —

note correct way to lay fire.

Fig. 21. Laying a Fire

if the tinder is damp. Small pieces of wood or other fuel can be laid gently on the kindling before lighting, or can be added as the kindling begins to burn. Add larger pieces of fuel when the kindling pile is considered large enough to support and ignite them. Don't pack the wood so tight that the draught is shut off. Encourage the fire by blowing gently on it.

61. For a large fire, the sticks in each layer should be parallel to each other and at right angles to the layer below. Space the sticks so that the air can get between them and create a good draught. For a small fire lay the sticks in radial fashion, and as they burn push them into the fire. With this method longer sticks need not be chopped up.

Emergency Fire Lighting

62. The availability of fire-lighting equipment may mean success or failure in a fight for survival. Many people have lost their lives because they have been unable to light a fire to provide warmth or attract attention. Your personal survival kit provides matches, candles, firemaking tablets, and a magnifying glass for this purpose.

63. Firemaking without matches requires bone-dry tinder which will burn very easily. Very dry powdered wood, finely shredded dry bark, cotton, twine, first-aid gauze bandage, fuzzy or woolly material scraped from plants, fine bird's feathers, or bird's nests are most suitable. You can make it burn more easily by adding a few drops of fuel.

64. **Burning Lens.** An emergency burning lens may be obtained from binoculars, gunsights, bombsights, or cameras. The lens should be used to focus the sun's rays on the timber.

65. Flint and Steel. A flint and steel is the easiest and most reliable way of making fire without matches. Your knife and sharpening stone or a piece of hard rock should produce a good spark. Hold the flint as near to the tinder as possible; strike it with a sharp scraping downward motion so that the sparks fall into the centre of the tinder.

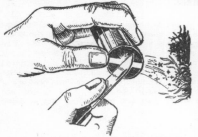

Fig. 22. Lighting a Fire with Flint and Steel

66. Bow Drill. Another standby is the bow drill. This consists of a bow made from a willow strung with some cord made from your parachute shroud lines. The drill is a circular shaft of dry wood around which the bow string is wound once. The drill shaft is pointed at one end and round at the other. The round end revolves in a depression made in a piece of wood which is held in one hand. Lubricate this depression. The point of the drill is placed in a notch in another piece of wood, which is filled with tinder. By holding the drill shaft in position and moving the bow

Note notch.

Fig. 23. Bow and Drill Method of Firemaking

79

back and forth in a sawing motion in a horizontal plane, friction is set up and the tinder ignited.

57. Pyrotechnic. A pyrotechnic may have to be used to light a fire if all other means have failed. Weigh the use of the pyrotechnic as an emergency signal against the need of a fire. The powder extracted from a pyrotechnic will burn so quickly that it will be necessary to mix a slower burning material with it; powdered wood or shredded fabrics are the best mixing materials. The powder from one pyrotechnic will provide sufficient tinder for a number of fires. The unused powder should be kept dry. Above all, **be extremely careful when you are extracting the powder from the pyrotechnic.**

Stockpile

68. Make all your preparations as far ahead as possible, regardless of whether or not you have been located. Stockpile fuel against bad weather or shortages. Stack it where it cannot be lost by drifting snow and protect it from rain. Prepare your kindling at least three fires ahead and store it inside your shelter.

Improvised Stoves

69. Aircraft fuels such as rubber, wax insulation, fuel and oil are more economically burned in improvised stoves. These stoves can be used inside or outside the shelter as required. To burn petrol, place one or two inches of sand or fine gravel in a tin or similar container and saturate it with petrol. Make slots at the top of the can to let the flames and smoke out and punch holes just above the level of the sand to provide a draught. To make the fire burn longer mix some oil with the petrol. If you have no container dig a hole in the ground, fill it with sand or gravel and pour on the fuel. Be careful when lighting; the petrol may explode; protect your face and hands. Lubricating oil, kerosene, or animal fats will not burn directly, but you can use them with a wick arrangement. Make a wick of kapok, asbestos, rope, rag, etc., and support it in the oil with a wire frame. A very simple stove can be made by putting a candle in a ventilated tin can. This will provide all the heat required for a snow shelter. (Figs. 24 and 25.)

Fig. 24.
Improvised Petrol Stove

Fig. 25.
Improvised Stove using Wick
to burn Oil or Animal Fat

Ventilation

70. The need for proper ventilation cannot be over-emphasized. When open fires or stoves are burned inside shelters, carbon monoxide and other gases will accumulate unless the shelter is ventilated. Also if animal fats or oil are burned, good ventilation will carry away the heavy black smoke. If a vent is made in the lower portion of the shelter—the entrance should be sufficient— and another at the top, cold air will move in through the lower opening, be warmed, and pass out through the top vent. The current of air will carry away the carbon monoxide and soot. Remember that carbon monoxide is heavier than air and a man lying down will be first affected. To retain the maximum amount of heat in a shelter restrict the vent holes when fires are out. *Restrict the temptation to "get up a good fug".*

FOOD

71. Take stock of all your available food. Your emergency food packs and uneaten flying rations are your immediate, and in the barren lands probably your only, sources of food. Your

food pack has been designed to provide sustenance for three days' very hard work, five days' active work, or seven days' normal work. The food packs contain their own directions of how they should be used. In extreme cold, two hot meals a day are necessary; one for breakfast and the other in the evening. Also, if you have enough, a hot drink at midday is desirable. Avoid drinking two hours before bedding down and remember to urinate immediately before getting into your sleeping bag.

Living Off the Land

72. Contrary to general belief, food is not abundant in the Arctic. All wild life is migratory and, since neither the time nor the position of the crash can be predetermined, there is no point in attempting to take up the involved subject of seasonal game distribution. The game you get in survival will either be there or come there. It means that you should survey the locality, set suitable traps, and wait for the game to come. To get food from the land you will have to do some very determined foraging. Leave a man in the camp at all times as look-out, while the rest of the party searches for food; detail men for fishing or hunting according to their talents. Care should be taken to blaze a trail back to camp. In large aircraft you might be carrying some sort of firearm, but you will normally have to rely on the snares and fishing kits in your survival packs. Additional snares may be made from wire and parachute elastics salvaged from the crash. You will have to learn where to look, what to look for, and, in all except plant food, how to catch it. When you find local animal or plant food, eat as much as you want and save your emergency rations. Fat is heat-producing food and very important to your health in the Arctic. Eat a lot of fat only when you can drink at least two pints of water daily. If you have any doubt about the safety of any wild food use the following rule: eat a spoonful and wait eight hours; if there are no ill effects, such as vomiting or diarrhoea, eat a handful and wait another eight hours. If there are still no ill effects, you can eat reasonable quantities safely.

Animal Food

73. Finding animals on the open tundra is not easy, but don't be too quick in deciding that the area is lifeless. Keep on the lookout for any signs of animal life—such as excrement, tracks,

hair, and, in extremely cold weather, "animal smoke" steaming from their bodies. These may put you on the trail of food. Wherever there is one kind of animal there are almost sure to be other forms of life. The animals you may find range from lemmings, which are stub-tailed mice, to polar bears. What you catch will depend on your facilities and skill. Small animals such as lemmings, muskrats, hares, woodchucks, squirrels, and snowshoe rabbits, can be caught with sling shots, snares, deadfalls, and other simple traps. The larger animals such as polar and brown bears, caribou, moose, seals, mountain sheep, and wolverine, are difficult to kill. They may be snared or captured by deadfalls and pit traps, but unless they are strangled or stunned they are hard to kill without a gun. Learn to attract animals by kissing the back of your hand vigorously and making a squeaking noise which indicates the presence of a wounded mouse or bird; that should definitely attract some hungry animal. But learn to conceal yourself.

Fig. 26. Simple Deadfall

Fig. 27. Tripwire Deadfall

Fig. 28. Simple Snare

Fig. 29. Trigger Snare

83

74. **Hunting Hints.**

(a) Keep the wind in your face. A calm day is not generally windless; make sure of the wind direction.

(b) Try to have the sun in your back, especially a rising or setting sun.

(c) In timber country move slowly and carefully; don't break any twigs under foot or allow swinging branches to hit your clothing.

(d) In hilly and mountainous country big game animals generally watch below them more than above. Keep slightly above the level where the game is most likely to be seen.

(e) In mountainous country, cross currents make it less important to keep the wind in your face.

(f) Animals are used to rolling stones in the mountains, therefore it is not quite so important to avoid noise.

(g) Avoid crispy snow; try to hunt where snow is soft.

(h) Don't expose yourself against a skyline.

(j) Never stay on the game trail; all wild game watch their back trails.

(k) If game is feeding, you can attempt to approach it by stalking in the open. Crawl slowly when all heads are down. Freeze motionless—whatever your position—the instant an animal starts to raise its head.

(l) When shooting game aim for the vital areas: behind the ears, in the throat, or behind the foreshoulders. Much game is lost because it is out of range.

75. **Poisonous Animals.** The liver of polar bears and bearded seals is poisonous at certain times of the year and should not be eaten. Rabbits are generally so lean and have so little food value that to get enough energy out of them you have to eat a little too much for comfort. Try to supplement your diet with other things.

Bird Food

76. Many northern birds nest in colonies which may run to hundreds of thousands of pairs. Near such a colony a man can keep alive—even without a gun. Some Arctic birds are well

supplied with fats—notably ducks, geese, and swans. These water birds all go through a two- or three-week flightless period while they are moulting in midsummer. The best known winter birds are the ptarmigan or snow partridge, which is rarely fat; the white owl, which is usually fat and tasty; and the raven, which is tough. All birds are good to eat cooked or raw. Their blood and livers are edible. The feathers can be used for insulation. The entrails and toes make good bait.

77. **Bird Catching.** Study bird habits closely. Hunt for birds on their meeting grounds on islands, cliffs, marshes and lakes, on coastal plains, and on flats in interior areas. An improvized slingshot is a good bird catcher. Ptarmigan are very tame and can be killed with a stick or stone. Gulls can be caught with a gorge hook and line; bait the hook and let it float on a piece of wood or stake it out on a beach. Eskimos set a simple noose snare in the nest itself to catch the bird's feet.

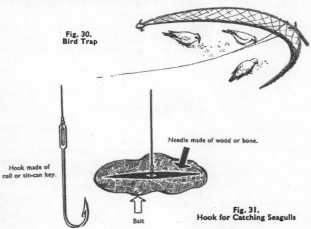

Fig. 30.
Bird Trap

Hook made of
nail or tin-can key.

Needle made of wood or bone.

Bait

Fig. 31.
Hook for Catching Seagulls

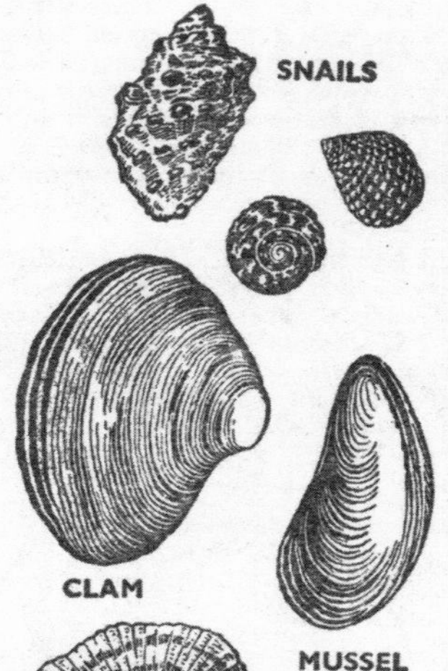

SNAILS

CLAM

MUSSEL

LIMPETS

Fig. 32.   CHITON Edible Seafood

Fish Food

78. The deeper streams, rivers, lakes, and tidal pools are all worth fishing. Along most Arctic shores clams, mussels, snails, limpets, chitons, sea urchins, and sea cucumbers, are plentiful. Don't eat shellfish that you find dead. Live shellfish move when touched or cling tightly to the rocks. The small blackish-purple mussel in Northern Pacific waters is poisonous at certain times of the year and should not be eaten. The chief characteristics of poisonous fish is that they lack ordinary scales, and instead have either a naked skin or are encased in a bony box-like covering or are covered with bristles, spiney scales, strong sharp thorns, or spines. Others puff up like a balloon on being taken out of the water. Cooking does not destroy the poisonous alkaloids in these fish. Never eat a fish that has slimy gills, sunken eyes, flabby flesh or skin, or an unpleasant odour. If on pressing the thumb against the fish it remains deeply dented, the fish is probably stale and should not be eaten. Avoid all types of jelly fish.

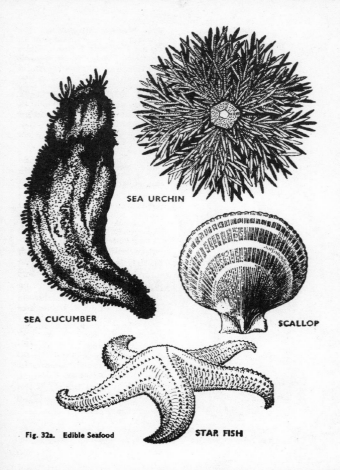

SEA URCHIN

SEA CUCUMBER

SCALLOP

Fig. 32a. Edible Seafood

STAR FISH

Fig. 33. Improvised Fish-hooks   88

79. Fishing Equipment. The fishing gear in your survival kit is not your only means of catching fish. They can be speared, caught in improvised nets, or stunned with sticks and stones. In shallow water you can even catch them with your hands. Those who have a fish net, or know how to make one and use it properly, will catch the most fish. Remember that a net works twenty-four hours a day.

80. Line Fishing. In addition to your fishing kit, hooks can be made from stiff wire or tin openers, and lines from the inner cords of your parachute shroud lines. Another effective device is a fishing needle of wood or bone sunk in bait (see Fig. 31). The needle is swallowed whole and a pull on the line swings it crosswise, causing it to catch in the fish's stomach or gullet. Use the least appetising parts of animals and birds for bait. A white stone used for a sinker, or a bit of shiny metal or brightly coloured piece of material tied just above the hook will also attract fish.

(a) **Jigging.** Fish may be caught by jigging for them. Let the hook, or a cluster of hooks attached below a "spoon" or shiny metal, down into deep water. Jerk it upwards at arm's length, and let it sink back. If you are fishing in deep water, be sure the hooks are weighted enough to carry the lure downwards quickly so that it suggests something alive.

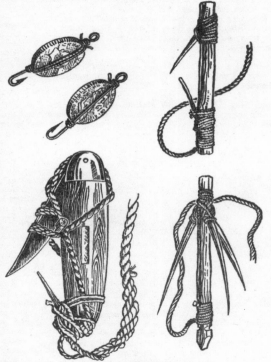

Fig. 33a. Improvised Fish-hooks

81. **Narrowing a Stream.** To catch fish, a shallow stream may be narrowed by building an obstruction of stones or stakes out from both banks, leaving only a narrow channel through which the fish can swim. An improvized net is stretched across this channel; be sure to secure it firmly with stakes or boulders or you will lose both net and fish. If you have no net, you can stand ready to hit, spear, or trap, the fish as they swim past. Keep very still while you wait—fish dart away at the first sign of danger.

82. **Diverting a Stream.** If you are certain that a small stream has fish in it, divert it and so strand fish in the pools in the stream below the diversion.

83. **Tidal Fish Trap.** To strand fish when the tide goes out, pile up a crescent of boulders on the tidal flat. Scooping out the area inside the crescent is not essential, but increases the effectiveness of the trap.

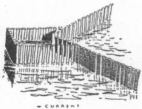

MAZE TYPE FISH TRAP   TIDAL FLAT FISH TRAP

Fig. 34. Tidal Fish Traps

84. **White Fish Traps.** If you come across a lagoon, select a spot about eight feet from it and two feet below water level. Dig a hole four feet in diameter, and join the hole to the lagoon with a trench about two feet wide, and deep enough to allow four inches of water to flow easily through the channel from the lagoon. Place a small log about three inches in diameter where the channel drops into the hole and fill the trench in behind it to smooth the

channel bed. Sit where the fish cannot see you and wait. Soon the fish will feel the current and, thinking that it will be taking them out to sea, allow it to carry them over the artificial falls into your pools.

85. **Fish in Tidal Pools.** Tidal pools with masses of seaweed in them may seem to contain no fish, but you may find small fish among the seaweed near the surface and a few big ones deeper down. For the small fish you will need a scoop or net. For the big ones use a spear or fish catcher.

86. **Fishing through Ice.** The main deterrent when attempting to fish through ice is thickness of the ice; it may be as much as 12 feet thick. Fishing with a hook and line through a hole in the ice requires no special technique, but setting a net beneath ice requires skill and patience. To set a net under ice, the float line may be fed under the ice by using a series of holes in the ice, one or two long poles, and a leader line tied to the float line. Fish get caught by entangling themselves in the mesh, therefore the net should be fairly loosely tied to the float line to allow some flexibility

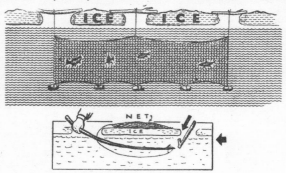

Method of placing net under ice.

Fig. 35. Setting Net under Ice

in the meshes. The net may be supported in the water by a combination of poles, floats, and ropes. Weights, made of almost anything, should be tied on to the bottom line.

Plant Food

87. Though plant food is not abundant in the Arctic, it is by no means absent. There are many varieties of berries, greens, roots, fungi, lichens, and seaweeds, which can be used as emergency food. In forested areas, food plants are most abundant in clearings, and along streams and seashores. On the tundra they are largest and most plentiful in wet places. Don't be discouraged by the bare appearance of northern vegetation; food is often hidden. Watch the feeding habits of animals, particularly birds; they will lead you to plants you might otherwise overlook. If you are on the march, gather food plants as you go along so that you will have enough for a meal by the time you make camp.

88. **Poisonous Plants.** Generally speaking, do not eat plants which taste bitter or have a milky sap. The following poisonous plants grow in the sub-Arctic forests; they do not normally grow north of the tree line:—

Fig. 36. Deathcup Amanita —Poisonous

(a) **Mushrooms.** The common characteristics of the two species of poisonous mushrooms are that they have white gills and swollen or bulbous bases. The nutritive value of mushrooms is very small, and unless you are an expert they are best left well alone. There is a possibility that the very young of the deadly amanita mushroom family may be mistaken for a puff ball. By cutting the ball in half you can make certain. If gills are found inside throw it away: no true puff balls have gills.

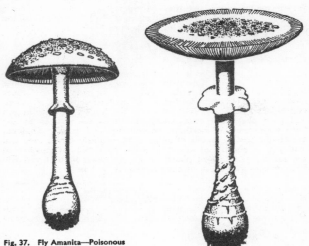

Fig. 37.   Fly Amanita—Poisonous

(b) *Water Hemlock.*   The water hemlock grows in the wet soil of river valleys in forested areas.   On an average the plant is four feet tall, but in favourable locations it grows to six to eight feet tall.   The arrangement of the flowers is a conspicuous characteristic which enables you to recognize immediately the members of this family (the parsley or carrot family).   The root is hollow and has cross partitions.   The leaves are streaked with purple and when crushed emit a disagreeable odour.   (Fig. 38.)

(c) *Baneberry.*   The berries are usually red or white but may turn blue as they get older.   It can be distinguished from the edible blueberry by the fact that baneberry bushes carry their fruits in clusters and have big leaves made up of several parts; edible blueberries grow singly.   (Fig. 39.)

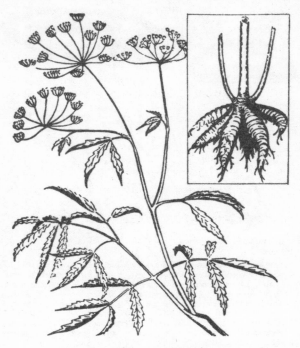

Fig. 38. Water Hemlock—Poisonous

Fig. 39. Baneberry—Poisonous

Cooking

89. Whenever possible, cook your food before eating it. Meals should be prepared in sheltered places. Windbreaks and large stones should be used to protect the flame and reflect the heat. Hot embers provide the most heat.

90. Since fuel is usually scarce, it is advisable to cook by means of boiling, and if possible drink the cooking water. Boiling in water is the easiest and most satisfactory method of preparing fish and game under survival conditions. Boiling preserves the essential elements of the food. It is best to boil sea food in sea water; no additional salting is then required. Undercook rather than over-cook; it saves vitamins and heat. Boil for two or three minutes only. Plant foods should be mixed with other foods in stews and soups. Lichens are most edible when soaked overnight, dried until brittle, crushed into a powder, and then boiled until they form a jelly. The jelly will make an excellent base for any soup or stew.

91. When a cooking pot is not available, in winter the food may be roasted or fried over a slow, non-smoking fire; in summer the food is best cooked by wrapping it in clay or mud and wet leaves, and baked in hot embers. When food is baked it should not be skinned or cleaned until it is cooked.

92. If no fire is available food becomes more palatable if dried or frozen. Before eating frozen food it should be brought to a temperature a few degrees below freezing since, when very cold, the frozen food sticks to the lips and tongue. When carved or sliced into thin shavings, it is really palatable and does not appear raw.

Food Storage

93. Your food supply—especially fresh meat—will attract thieving animals. Another problem is the alternate freezing and thawing which is bad for any food. In winter let your food freeze and stay frozen until you need it. It is not necessary to thaw before cooking. Frozen food may take a little longer to cook, but other-wise it is unaffected. In summer, your fish can be cut into strips and dried in the sun; meat and game should be kept in a cool

place in the shade. Newly-killed meat or game should be tied in a parachute cloth to keep out flies which otherwise will lay eggs on the meat. A hole dug in the shady side of an embankment, with a wet piece of heavy material hung over the entrance, will give a small degree of refrigeration. A hole dug in the ground similarly covered will also make a good refrigerator. On the tundra a common method of storing food is to place it beneath a pile of boulders. If boulders are not available bury your food in the snow, and mark the spot. In timbered country, if it becomes necessary for every one to be away from the camp (one man should be left to operate the emergency signals) don't leave the food where animals can reach it. Tie it in a bundle and hang it from a tree at least six feet from the ground and a foot or two from the branches.

WATER

94. Your water supply will be limited only by the amount of heat available for melting snow and ice. In an effort to save fuel men deprive themselves of drinking water. Inefficiency, exhaustion and dehydration may occur through lack of water, even in the Arctic. Drink if possible two pints of water daily. The water lost through the sweat glands, and in the form of urine, must be replaced. The amount of water lost in the form of sweat, and therefore your requirements, can be limited by regulating your rate of work and removing some of your clothing whenever you begin to feel warm.

95. In summer, water can be obtained from streams, lakes, or ponds. On the tundra, pond water may be brown because of stain from grass roots and other plants, but it is fit to drink.

96. In winter, your water supply is most easily obtained from lakes under the ice and snow. The lower surface of the ice follows the contours of the top surface of the snow; dig where the snow is deepest and then chip through the ice under this to find the least cold water. Melt ice rather than snow for water; you will get more water for volume and it takes less time and heat. The deeper layers of snow are more granular and give a better yield of water then the soft upper snow. When melting snow, place

a small amount in the pot at first, adding more as it melts. If you fill the pot with snow, the first water will be soaked up by the absorbent snow above it, leaving a cavity directly over the heated bottom of the pot and the pot will burn.

97. At sea you can obtain good drinking water from old sea ice. Ice a year old rarely has any noticeable saltiness, while ice two or three years' old is generally fresher than the average river or spring water. Old sea ice can be distinguished from the current year's ice by its rounded corners and bluish colour, in contrast to the rougher sea ice which has a milky grey colour. In summer, drinking water can be obtained from pools in the old sea ice. Avoid pools near the edge of the floe where salt water may have blown in.

98. **Purification of Water.** If there is any doubt as to the quality of the water you intend to drink or cook with, it should be purified by one of the following methods:—

(a) *Halazone Tablets.* Crunch and dissolve one halazone tablet in each pint of water. Shake well and allow to stand for half-an-hour. If this is insufficient to produce a distinct smell of chlorine, add more halazone until the odour is present.

(b) *Boiling.* Boil the water for at least three minutes and allow any sediment to settle before using.

HEALTH HAZARDS

Hypothermia

99. Hypothermia is the condition existing when the body temperature is below normal. Low temperature, winds, and dampness, supplement each other in depleting the body's heat resources to produce a sub-normal temperature. Hypothermia may be recognized by decreasing resistance to cold, excessive shivering, and low vitality.

100. The treatment consists of returning the body temperature to normal. The patient should be put in his sleeping bag, or a bed improvized from a parachute canopy, the buttocks, shoulders, and feet, being well insulated. The patient should be warmed by

placing heated rocks, wrapped in some material, near the various parts of the body. If the number of heating units is limited place them as far as they will go in this order: pit of the stomach, small of the back, armpits, back of the neck, wrists, and between the thighs. Stimulation with hot drinks will also help if the patient is conscious. Avoid the use of alcohol; it opens the blood vessels at the surface of the skin allowing heat to be lost more rapidly. A victim of hypothermia is not cured when his body temperature returns to normal. Build up his reserve of body heat. To prevent hypothermia take all possible measures to conserve body heat.

Frostbite

101. **Areas Most Affected.** Frostbite affects particularly the exposed parts of the body and regions which are farthest from the heart and have the least blood circulation, *i.e.* the face, nose, ears, hands, and feet.

102. **Prevention.** To avoid frostbite remember these precautions:—

(*a*) Keep wrinkling your face to make sure that stiff patches have not formed. Watch your hands.

(*b*) Watch each others' faces and ears for signs of frostbite.

(*c*) Don't handle cold metal with bare hands.

(*d*) Avoid tight clothing which will reduce circulation and increase the risk of frostbite.

(*e*) Avoid exposure in high winds.

(*f*) Avoid spilling petrol on bare flesh. Petrol-splashed flesh in sub-zero temperatures will freeze almost at once.

(*g*) Do not go out of your shelter, even for short periods, without adequate clothing.

(*h*) Take special care if you are unfit or fatigued; the risk then increases.

(*j*) Don't let your clothing become wet from sweat or water. If it does, dry it promptly.

(a) Frostbite first appears as a small patch of white or cream-coloured frozen skin, which is firm to the touch and feels stiff. Frostbite can be felt by making faces and moving all the skin on the face and forehead. The subject may feel a slight

Fig. 40.   Making Faces to Prevent Frostbite

pricking sensation as the skin freezes, or may not notice it at all. If treatment is given at this stage the consequences will not be serious; but if the process goes further, the deeper tissues of muscle and bone are frozen, the blood vessels become clotted, and so much tissue may be destroyed that part of a limb, an ear, or a nose, may be lost.

(b) If the frostbite is quite mild, when the area is warmed up, there will be some swelling and redness of the skin with a little pain and, as the condition heals, the skin may scale off.

(c) If the bite is deeper and more serious, swelling and pain are marked and blisters form. These may become infected, forming ulcers, and in the worst case the tissues become grey, then black and dead. Such tissues will fall off eventually.

104. **Treatment.** Careful and immediate attention must be given.

(a) Very slight cases may be treated by simply getting out of the wind. A small area may be warmed by placing a bare hand over it, covering the outside of the hand with its mitt. The woollen pads on the backs of the mitts may provide enough warmth in some cases.

(b) Frostbitten hands should be thrust inside your clothing against your body.

(c) Frostbitten feet should be thrust inside a companion's clothing if you are out in the open.

(d) Keep the part covered with dry clothing until you reach shelter.

(e) Never rub frostbite with snow.

(f) In more serious cases the patient will almost certainly require treatment for exposure. Get him to shelter or build a shelter round him.

(g) If blisters appear, do not burst them. Dust them with an antiseptic powder.

(h) Cover the frostbitten parts lightly with surgical dressings, or clean soft clothes. Wrap up the parts loosely.

(i) Never rub a frostbitten area.

(k) Never warm up frostbite quickly by holding before the fire or dipping into hot water, or by any other means. Use "animal" warmth only.

(l) If there is severe pain give morphia if available. Very severe pain is usually an indication that the frostbitten parts have been made too hot and further damage is occurring.

(m) Keep the damaged areas at rest.

Snow Blindness

105. Snow blindness is a temporary form of blindness caused by the high intensity and concentration of the sun's rays, both direct and reflected, from the snow-covered ground or ice and ice crystals in the clouds. However, snow blindness may occur during a bright overcast when there is no direct light, but a bright general haze from all directions. It occurs most frequently when the sun is high, particularly in areas which do not lose their snow cover.

106. Symptoms. First the eyes become sensitive to the glare, then blinking and squinting occurs. Next the landscape takes on a pinkish tinge and the eyes begin to water. Blinking and watering become more intense and the vision becomes redder, until a sensation similar to that of sand in the eyes is noticed. If the exposure is continued the sensation becomes more violent until the vision is blanked out completely by a flaming red curtain. It is impossible to open the eyes or to black the red vision. There is intense pain which may last three or four days.

107. Treatment. The treatment consists of getting the person into a dark place. If there is no dark place available a blindfold may be used. The pain is aggravated by heat and may be relieved by the application of a cool wet compress. Time is the only cure.

108. Prevention. The wearing of the standard goggles in the personal survival kit is recommended. If for some reason you have no goggles, some kind of goggles can be made from wood, bark, cloth or paper; do not use metal. Blackening the skin round the eyes will cut down the number of rays entering the eyes.

Fig. 41. Protection against Snow blindness

Carbon Monoxide Poisoning

109. All forms of fires and stoves are liable to give off carbon monoxide gas, and are therefore a potential danger in shelters unless ventilation is adequate (*see* para. 70). Poisoning by these fumes is common in severe cold conditions because of the very natural tendency to batten down closely. The gas is colourless and odourless.

110. The effects of breathing the gas are insidious. There may be slight headache, dizziness, drowsiness, nausea, and perhaps vomiting, but usually these symptoms are very mild and may pass unnoticed, and the subject becomes unconscious without any warning. Unless discovered promptly the subject will die as the effects of the gas increase.

111. The treatment is simple. Remove the patient to a well-ventilated place and encourage him to breath evenly and regularly. If he is unconscious and breathing shallowly, apply artificial respiration. Administer oxygen if available. When he is conscious keep him warm and at rest and give hot drinks. Do not allow him to exert himself until he is fully recovered.

Personal Hygiene

112. Strict attention must be paid to personal cleanliness to prevent skin and intestinal infections which are associated with neglect of personal hygiene.

(*a*) Hair and beards should be trimmed as short as possible. Frost accumulates readily on beards and can only be removed by thawing.

(*b*) Winter survival is not conducive to bathing; however, it is still necessary to remove accumulated body oils and perspiration from the skin. Under severe conditions a dry rub-down is all that is possible; otherwise wash the body with a damp rag.

(*c*) The teeth and mouth should be cleaned daily. Feathers make a good toothpick and several tied together make a reasonable toothbrush. A piece of cloth can also be used.

(*d*) Attend promptly to any tender skin, particularly on the feet. It may prevent real trouble later on.

Camp Hygiene

113. Use a little commonsense when arranging your camp site. Site your lavatory to the leeward of the camp, well away from your shelter and water supply. Clean the camp site regularly, and above all do not contaminate your water supply.

General Health

114. Conserve your energy. Do not rush around aimlessly. Avoid fatigue. Get plenty of sleep. If you cannot sleep, just lie down and relax your body and mind. You will not freeze to death when you sleep unless you are utterly exhausted. If you are doing hard work remove excess clothing before you get hot, and rest as soon as you begin to feel hot, or at least for five minutes in every thirty.

CLOTHING PRECAUTIONS

115. It has previously been stated that your clothing is your first line of defence in Arctic survival, and it follows that care of the clothing is most important. The following points should be particularly observed.

116. **Regulation and Ventilation.** Strange as it may seem, one of the chief causes of freezing to death arises from having become overheated in the first place. Excess body vapour will condense and in extreme cases will freeze. This has two effects: the moisture will destroy the insulating qualities of the underclothing, and the water vapour, being a good conductor of heat, will draw heat from the body. Constantly regulate your clothing so that you do not become hot enough to sweat. This is a considerable nuisance, but absolutely necessary. Slacken off all draw cords, open up the clothing at the neck, and loosen belts to allow ventilation. When necessary, remove enough layers of clothing to keep cool, whether you are indoors or travelling, or working outdoors. Replace the clothing as soon as you start to cool off.

117. **Repairs.** Immediately mend tears and holes, particularly in outer garments which must be windproof.

118. Drying Out. Dry your garments as soon as possible if they have become wet. Clothing should be hung high up in shelters to dry, as the warmest air is high up. In emergency, clothing can be dried by body heat, by putting it under your outer clothing or inside your sleeping bag. Mukluks and boucherons should be dried in the open by sublimation, that is, allowing the perspiration to condense and then freeze. The frozen perspiration can then be brushed out.

119. Fluffing Out. Compression reduces the fluffiness of a material and hence the volume of insulating air it can contain. Socks must be turned frequently and fluffed out to prevent matting. Insoles should be changed from foot to foot to prevent them always being compressed in the same spot. All other woollen garments should be fluffed out regularly.

120. Spares for Changing. If possible carry extra dry clothing for changing, particularly socks. Several layers of the parachute canopy wrapped round your feet are better than wet socks. Dry grass stuffed between the layers provides useful insulation.

121. Frost Removal. Remove snow and hoar frost from clothing by beating, shaking and scraping, before entering a warmer atmosphere. Willow canes or a whisk made of spruce tips can be used for this purpose. Snow or frost does not wet clothing unless it is melted by warmth, so if you cannot remove the snow it is better to leave the outer garments where it is cold, so that the snow will not melt.

122. Snow Contact. Don't sit down directly on the snow. Your body heat will melt it and your clothing will become wet. Always sit on surplus clothing, a log, or some piece of equipment. Don't put your hands with snow-covered gloves into your pockets. Shake off the snow first.

123. Tightness of Clothing. Avoid tight clothing, particularly tight footgear and handwear. Don't try to cram too many pairs of socks into your footgear, because a tight fit is as bad as, if not worse than, insufficient covering.

124. Cleanliness. Keep all your clothing as clean as possible. Dirty, matted clothing is less warm. The dirt will fill the space normally occupied by the insulating air.

125. Gloves. Don't lose your gloves or mittens. Secure them, by the loops provided, with a neck string.

126. Taking Chances. Don't take chances about clothing. Unprotected fingers and ears can be frostbitten in a few minutes.

127. Sleeping Bags. Never get into your sleeping bag wearing wet clothing. Sleep in the minimum clothing required for warmth; naked if possible. Turn the bag inside out in the morning and dry it before a fire or by sublimation. When it is dry, reassemble it and roll it up tightly until it is needed again. Don't sleep with your head in the bag, otherwise moist exhaled air will enter the bag. Sleep with your head in the aperture, and cover your face with your necksquare folded up to at least four thicknesses.

128. Clothing Hints.

(a) When walking in deep snow, wear your trousers outside your footwear and secure the bottoms of the legs with the draw cords.

(b) If you are unfortunate enough to fall into water, immediately roll yourself in the snow. The snow will act as a blotter and soak up the water. The violent exercise will generate body heat and will also knock off any saturated snow. If possible wring out underclothing, but let the outer clothing freeze to maintain and protect body heat.

(c) Never take off boots filled with water until you are in some form of shelter. As long as water remains liquid there is no danger of frostbite. Walking generates enough heat to prevent solidification for a considerable time even at very low temperatures.

(d) Footwear can be made temporarily waterproof by dipping them, while on the feet, into water, until a film of ice is formed on the outside. The footwear will not let in water until the ice has melted. Coating with ice is an extreme emergency procedure and should never be used if there are other alternatives.

INSECTS

129. From mid-June to mid-September, when the first heavy frosts come, your worst enemies are the insects. During this period, there are ten times as many mosquitos per square mile over two-thirds of the land north of the tree line than in the tropics. Hence the provision of the head net and insect repellant cream in your personal survival kit.

130. There are four insect families: mosquitos, black flies, deer flies, and midges. They do not resemble each other in general appearance, but they are alike in several significant ways:

(a) They all bite, that is, they do not sting.

(b) They do not generally carry disease.

(c) They are primarily daytime insects.

(d) If it turns cold, they become inactive, even when they are abundant.

(e) Only the females bite.

(f) During their larval stage they live in water.

Types

131. (a) *Mosquitos.* Mosquitos need no description; they are universal pests.

(b) *Black Flies.* Sometimes known as sandflies or buffalo gnats. Their bites stay open and will continue to bleed for some time; the bite causes severe swelling. They attack especially at the collar line, and, if they get inside the clothing, at the waist line.

(c) *Deer Flies.* These large pests are also known as gadflies. Other flies in the same family are mooseflies; these are larger still and are also called horseflies or bulldogs. The last name is particularly apt in view of their tenacity and the size of the hole they drill in the skin. Their bite is like the cut of a scalpel, drawing blood in a trickle.

(d) *Midges.* These are minute flies about one twenty-fifth of an inch long; also known as no-see-ums, pinkies, and gnats. They are persistent blood suckers and cause a sharp, burning pain out of all proportion to their size.

Protection

132. **Clothing.** Wear two thicknesses of light clothing: mosquitos bite through one layer but rarely through two. Tuck your trouser legs in your boots and your sleeves in your gloves. Whenever you can, cover bare flesh with clothing.

133. **Headnets.** Make sure your headnet is well tucked in to the collar of the shirt.

134. **Insect Repellant.** Apply to the face and exposed skin every four hours. Apply to the face even when wearing a headnet; midges are small enough to penetrate the mesh.

135. **Smudge Fires.** Any green wood or green leaves will produce an insect repelling smoke.

136. **Parachute Canopies.** In summer, the aircraft may be used as a shelter and can be made insect-proof with parachute canopies.

TRAVEL

137. The experience of Arctic crashes reveals that the best policy for survivors is to stay with the crashed aircraft and await rescue. Travel to a camp site should be undertaken, however, if the scene of the crash is endangered by natural hazards, such as crevasses and avalanches. There may be times when walking home is considered to be the only solution.

Considerations

138. **Your Position.** Have you been able to fix your position? Quite often the reason for crash landing is that the aircraft is lost. An approximate position, say within 50 miles, is worthwhile for the purpose of narrowing the search by air. But it is not accurate enough to use as a departure point in an attempt to walk out. You must know the exact location of your camp and your objective.

139. **Wireless Contact.** Is the search organization aware of your plight and your position? Was your distress message acknowledged? Have you made wireless contact since the crash?

140. **Physical Condition.** Even with snow shoes and skis, Arctic travel is slow, strenuous, and hazardous. Don't overestimate your physical capabilities.

141. **Weather.** The weather should be assessed from two angles. Is the prevailing weather likely to hinder search forces? Is the weather conducive to an Arctic route-march and sleep in temporary shelters?

142. **Orientation.** You must have reliable methods of determining and maintaining your intended route. In the barren lands particularly, you must have a compass. Should you lose your compass the following methods may be used to determine direction:—

(*a*) *Sky Map.* A high uniform overcast reflects the surrounding terrain. Clouds over open water, timber, or snowfree ground will appear black, while clouds over sea ice or uniform snow covering will appear white. Pack ice or drifted snow are indicated by a mottled appearance on the surface of the cloud. New ice is indicated by greyish patches on the sky map. A careful study of the earth's reflection on the clouds may be used for determining the proper direction to travel.

(*b*) *Bird Habits.* Migrating waterfowl fly towards the land in the thaw. Most sea birds fly out to sea in the morning and return to land at night.

(*c*) *Vegetation.* Although there are few trees on the tundra, the moss theory still applies; moss is heaviest on the north side. The bark of the alders is lighter in colour on the south side than on the north side. Don't rely on one observation; make several and average the direction. Lichens on rocks are most numerous on the south side, where they receive the greatest warmth of the sun.

(d) **Stars.** In the northern hemisphere, true north can be ascertained from the constellation of the Great Bear, which points to Polaris (North Star), the star over the North Pole. Trying to estimate your latitude by measuring the angle of Polaris above the horizon will give you only a very approximate result, unless you have a sextant and tables. In the southern hemisphere, the Southern Cross indicates the direction of south. Other constellations, such as Orion, rise in the east and set in the west, moving to the south of you when you are north of the equator and vice versa.

(e) **Sun.** If you have the correct local time on your watch, the shadow cast by an object at 1200 hours will indicate north and south. The object must be perpendicular to the ground and straight. In the northern hemisphere the base of the shadow will indicate south and the tip will indicate north. If you have no watch, place a straight object in the ground or snow on a level spot. Starting in the morning, and continuing about once every hour throughout the day, mark the point at the tip of the shadow. At the end of the day, connect these points and you will have a line which runs true east and west. The shortest distance between the base of the shadow and the east-west line will indicate north and south. The method of determining direction by pointing the hour hand of a watch at the sun is considered inaccurate and should not be used.

143. **Final Decision.** A crashed aircraft with a prominent signals area is more likely to be spotted from the air than a man on the march with limited signalling devices. Your final decision should be based on two factors: your nearness to civilization and the probability of rescue. Once you have made your decision, stick to it. This decision will have been reached after considering all the factors when your minds were fresh. As time goes on, your powers of reasoning will deteriorate and there may be a tendency to consider the factors individually instead of collectively. However, if it is at all possible, or if you are in any doubt, *stay with the aircraft.*

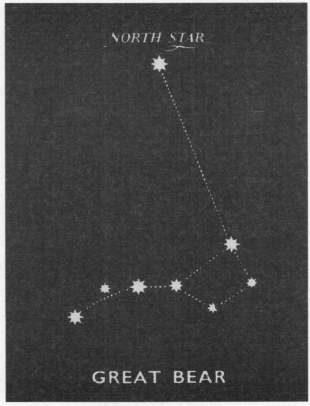

NORTH STAR

GREAT BEAR

Fig. 42. Great Bear and North Star

Fig. 43. Southern Cross

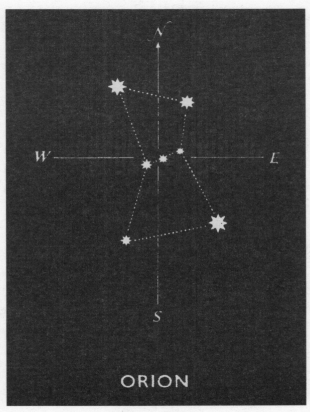

Fig. 44. Orion

113

Routes

144. The majority of the settlements are to be found on the rivers or on the coast. Water is the highway of the north. Dog teams and sledge trains travel on the ice in the winter. In addition, food and fuel are available along the waterways both in summer and winter. Travel downstream to reach civilization, except in Siberia where the rivers flow north.

145. **Mountain Routes.** Mountain routes, where ice caps, glaciers, crevasses, and avalanches may be encountered, are extremely hazardous and should be used only if there is no alternative. The minimum requirements are a climbing rope, two ice axes, and an experienced leader. If any one of these is not available select another route. In areas where avalanches are prevalent, travel in the early morning when it is coldest. At all times proceed with extreme caution.

146. **Timber Country.** Snow lies deep in timber country and travel is extremely difficult without snowshoes or skis. Two miles a day in these circumstances is good progress. Trail breaking is very strenuous, and it should be taken in turns for periods of not more than five minutes. Rest for five minutes about every half-an-hour. When possible travel by the rivers. Make a raft or use your dinghy in the summer, and travel on foot over the ice in winter. When travelling on river ice keep on the inside of the bends; the swifter current on the outside of the bends wears the ice away from below. At river junctions walk on the far side, or take to the land until you are well downstream from the junction. When river travel is not feasible, travel along ridges. In winter the snow does not lie deep on the ridges; in summer the ridges are drier and firmer under foot.

147. **Barren Land Routes.** Barren land travel without snowshoes or skis is difficult and slow. You cannot afford to follow the rivers, which wind and twist and greatly increase the distance to be covered. Beware of thin ice on the edges of tundra lakes and in the connecting channels. Lack of landmarks, blowing snow, and fog, emphasize the need of a compass for barren land travel. If your tracks are clear, check your course by taking back bearings of your tracks; otherwise proceed in single file about 30 paces

apart. The last man carries the compass and, using the middle men as sighting objects, controls the course of the first man by calling out instructions to him. Constant compass checks will ensure that you are travelling in a straight line, which is the shortest distance. Summer travel in the barren lands presents another problem. Soggy vegetation and bogs make the going slippery and heavy. Tundra lakes, quicksands, and swamps must be avoided. In these circumstances it is usually preferable to float down a river than to travel across country.

148. **Sea Ice Routes.** On sea ice travel in one party; there is nothing to be gained by anyone who remains behind. The problems of coursekeeping are identical with those on the barren lands, but the movement of ice floes makes it difficult to determine your actual track. Pressure ridges and hummocks may be used as landmarks over short distances only, since they are constantly moving. The unreliability of the magnetic compass in high latitudes necessitates course checks on the sun and stars. Avoid tall, pinnacled icebergs which are liable to capsize. For shelter at sea, look for low, flat-topped icebergs.

149. **Trail Equipment.** The amount of equipment you can take on the trail will depend on what you can carry, or haul on improvised sledges. Individual packs, adapted from the personal survival packs, should be worn high up on the shoulders and should not exceed a weight of 35 pounds. Avoid carrying whenever possible; float down the rivers in summer and haul a sledge in winter. Sledges can be made from cowlings, doors, pieces of fuselage, or timber. A single tow line attached to a bridle, with individual shoulder loops tied in, is preferable for travel over snow. Only one trail need necessarily be broken. Over ice, it is better to have several towlines attached to the bridle, since they enable each man to choose his own footholds. It may be necessary to leave behind many useful articles. Basically you will require food, shelter, and fuel, or means of obtaining them. The value of each piece of equipment must be carefully considered. For instance, a fuel stove is superfluous in timber country, but is an absolute necessity on sea ice. Always carry spare clothes and a sleeping bag. Travel is difficult over any terrain without snow-shoes or skis. Short wide skis are best; they should be about three

feet long and eight inches wide. They can be made of metal or timber. Snowshoes, which are simply load-spreaders, can be made of metal tubing, spruce, or willow. Finer limbs can be woven in and secured with shroud lines.

150. **Preparation.** While the advice to all survivors is *"Stay with the aircraft"*, the possibility of the necessity for travel should be recognized at the beginning of the survival period. Items of equipment such as snowshoes, skis, and sledges, should be made and tested before setting out on the trail. Indeed, they will be very useful around the camp site for collecting fuel and foraging for food.

151. **Blaze your Trail.** If the entire survival party is going to walk out, or if a small group is setting out to get help, messages stating the intended route should be left at the base camp. In the Arctic communication is very slow, and the more signs of your presence left along the trail the greater is your chance of being found. Mark your trail clearly. Strange trails are nearly always

Fig. 45. Trail Blazing

followed by trappers and Eskimos. On the trail make your camp well before nightfall; leave plenty of time to build your shelter, prepare emergency signals, and have a hot meal. The following morning, all signals, particularly snow writing, should be changed to large arrows showing the direction the party has taken.

152. Finally, it must again be strongly emphasized that if you are in any doubt at all **stay with the aircraft.**

E43541 Wt.38194-BN.3823 5,700 7/53 Gp.8 Fosh & Cross Ltd., London

JUNGLE

SURVIVAL

A.M. PAMPHLET 214 TROPICAL ISSUE

JUNGLE SURVIVAL

INTRODUCTION

1. There is no standard form of jungle and the word implies either wet tropical rain forest, which is the jungle we usually think about, or dry open scrub country ; it refers to any natural uncultivated forest in tropical or sub-tropical lands.

2. Jungle is not constant in composition even in the same climatic zones. Its vegetation depends on the altitude, and, to a large extent, on the influence of man through the centuries. Tropical trees take over 100 years to reach maturity and are only fully grown in untouched primeval virgin forest. This is called "primary" jungle and is easily recognized by its abundance of giant trees 150 feet to 200 feet high and up to 10 feet in width at the base. The tops of the trees form a dense carpet over 100 feet from the ground beneath which there is little light and therefore comparatively little undergrowth : consequently travel is not too difficult in most primary jungle and its animal inhabitants live mainly in the upper branches.

3. Jungle is not all primary. Far eastern hill tribesmen grow one rice crop a year by burning down a suitable area of jungle and planting seed in the ashes which form a natural fertiliser. When the harvest is gathered the tribe moves on to find a fresh jungle area to be burned for next year's crop. In this way one tribe will devastate large areas of primary jungle in a decade. European exploitation has added to the cleared area by felling accessible tall timber along river banks. The cleared area is soon reclaimed by the jungle, but by jungle without tall trees and composed of dense undergrowth and creepers. This is "secondary" jungle and it is much harder to traverse than primary jungle, but it is better for forced landing or parachute descent because of the absence of giant trees.

4. In most far eastern countries, the secondary jungle is greater in extent than the untouched primary jungle. The latter is now found only in the most inaccessible mountainous country or in

areas of forest reserve, preserved by colonial governments for water catchment or other reasons. Don't, however, believe that all the tropics consist of jungle of any sort. Well over half the land is cultivated in some way or other and you will find rubber plantations, tea plantations, coconut plantations, and native allotments. You should learn to recognize these from the air as they are a sure indication of human activities. Remember that neither rubber trees nor coconut palms grow wild in any quantity, and if the plantation is there then the planter cannot be far off. He may only be an isolated Malay but he has to sell his crop somewhere, so he will have good though infrequent contacts with civilization. Remember, too, that rubber trees must be tapped daily to draw off the valuable sap, so that if you get into a rubber plantation you will be found within 24 hours.

5. Primary or secondary, the tropical rain jungle is a difficult and unpleasant land to live in and travel through. The soil is covered with dead and rotting vegetation over which leeches move in countless millions. Numerous other slugs, insects, and small animal life will be found, all in some way loathsome and unpleasant. In low-lying country the ground may be marshy and even under water, with only the trees and their buttressed roots showing the presence of soil below. Close to the ground will be found thick, and, in secondary forests, sometimes impenetrable, undergrowth containing a considerable number of plants, fruits, and vegetables, some edible and some poisonous. Over the undergrowth in primary jungle is the rather more open space beneath the jungle tree tops, with an abundance of all types of trees, creepers, and vines amongst which you will sometimes see animal and bird life. Over all this is the thick jungle top or umbrella through which little light penetrates. Here amongst the tree tops may be found birds, bees, moths, monkeys, and so on. Yet, despite the teeming life of this jungle you may journey for several days and see no sign of it, so timid and shy are the majority of the inhabitants ; and, among all these living things, you may starve if you are not jungle-wise.

6. The dry scrub country is more open than the wet jungle, and prickly-pear, cactus, and leafless cactus-like trees are common amid the thorny brakes and tall grass. It is tiresome to be caught in this country, for its lack of topographical features, population and tracks, make it difficult to find a way out. But patience, a compass, and common sense will do the trick.

7. Despite all the perils and unpleasantness of the jungle, thousands of Englishmen have lived and travelled in it safely for months on end, and hundreds of them have enjoyed it and still do. With a little knowledge you can achieve safety if not enjoyment.

ESSENTIAL CHARACTERISTICS
OF THE "JUNGLE HIKER"

8. Whatever the type of country into which you are unfortunate enough to crash-land, or "bale-out", or if after a successful ditching you make a landfall on some small tropical island, your chances of survival and eventual rescue depend on a few definite factors. By far the most important of these is the first, "determination to live"; but together they will give you the morale to bring you through :—

    (a) Determination to live.

    (b) Previous knowledge; ignorance of a few simple rules on the part of one member of the party is a danger to the remainder.

    (c) Confidence in your knowledge of jungle and island life.

    (d) Common sense and initiative.

    (e) Discipline, and a previously considered plan of action.

    (f) Ability to learn by your mistakes.

ACTION DURING EMERGENCY

9. The ways of getting into the jungle are baling-out or crash-landing, and the decision will be dependent on the circumstances at the time of the emergency. But whichever course is chosen, on the way down, make a mental note of the following :—

    (a) The character of the country into which you are going. Consider the relative positions of rivers, lakes, clearings, paddy fields, high ground, ridges, villages, in fact anything which might be of use to you later on.

    (b) Try to pin-point yourself in relation to one of these, i.e. get a mental note of the bearing.

    (c) If baling-out into thick jungle, it will be vital that you should have some idea of the heading or bearing of the aircraft, or members of the crew in relation to each other, as once "in", it will be found extremely difficult to make contact if you have no knowledge of your relative positions.

To Jump or Not to Jump

10. If the terrain is at all suitable it is normally better to crash-land than to bale-out. However, if you are over mountainous country, or if the aircraft is on fire or out of control, a crash-landing

may be out of the question. To sum up, the advantages of staying with your aircraft are :—

(a) The crew is not separated and no member of it will be left alone. This is most desirable from the morale aspect.

(b) All the equipment in the aircraft will be available and it will be possible to improvize other essential items from airframe and engine parts.

(c) The fuselage, if intact, provides shelter from animals, insects, and weather.

(d) The aircraft or its wreckage is plainly visible from the air.

11. In contrast, baling-out offers only one distinct advantage, that is, the ability to get you down safely on almost any sort of country. However, try not to bale-out over primary jungle if you can avoid it, as you will almost certainly sustain some sort of injury when you land in the tree tops, and you may even find yourselves dangling twixt heaven and earth over a hundred feet from the ground.

12. For the reasons outlined above, if you have to bale-out over a jungle, try to arrange a rendezvous for the crew before you jump. The best rendezvous is your wrecked aircraft and you can decide on that action before you even take-off on a flight.

FORCED LANDING GROUNDS—
SUITABLE TERRAIN

13. The jungle does not offer much in the way of forced-landing areas, but if you have any choice or time to make a selection, consider the areas mentioned below, in order of preference :—

(a) Beaches.

(b) Clearings.

(c) Paddy fields—land along the "bunds", i.e. banks of mud dividing the fields.

(d) Lakes and rivers.

Do not land on tree tops—if it has to be the tree tops, bale-out if there is the height and time to carry out the drill, with due consideration to all those in the aircraft.

IMMEDIATE ACTION ON LANDING

14. The planning of a standard procedure is essential to the ultimate success of the incident, and the following immediate actions should be carried out after landing. This procedure or

drill is, of course, subsequent to the normal crash landing drills, precautions against fire, etc. : —

(a) *First Aid.* Administer immediate first aid to the slightest scratch. In hot and tropical climates the risk of poisoning from an open wound is very great.

(b) *Fix Position.* You cannot decide on a reliable plan of action until you have decided just where you are. You may not be able to fix your position to the nearest mile, but you must be able to say "I am within this area". If the aircraft is intact, use the sextant, chronometer, and altimeter to help fix your position.

(c) *Rendezvous if Scattered.* The place for rendezvous after parachute landing should normally be the wreckage of the aircraft. If the captain has sufficient time before ordering his crew to jump, he may decide to rendezvous at some geographical landmark. If so, he must ensure that all the crew know and can recognize the point of rendezvous and that the landmark is prominent, *e.g.* the confluence of two rivers.

(d) *Establish Two-way Radio Contact if Possible.* If the aircraft radio equipment is intact, try and contact the outside world on W/T or R/T. Erect an emergency aerial if necessary and run one of the engines to maintain power if you can do so without risk of fire.

(e) *Prepare all Signalling Gear for Immediate Use.* You will not have time to prepare signalling fires, etc., if you wait until you see aircraft searching for you. Have fires lighted in readiness for the search aircraft and keep oil and petrol near the fires so that you can produce a dense column of smoke at short notice. The petrol will make a rapid flare-up by night. Consider what steps can be taken to make the scene of the incident more noticeable from the air. Make a clearing for the display of ground signals (see page 68), or move to a clearing nearby if you can find one. Spread out parachutes and polished aluminium panels to reflect the sun. Try and evolve signalling methods which will show above the jungle top, *i.e.* smoke columns or parachutes spread over the trees.

(f) *Check Emergency Equipment, including Rations.* Check the survival equipment available from your personal kits and emergency packs. Examine the other equipment in the aircraft and decide what will be of use to you, *e.g.* fire axe, compasses, parachutes, etc. Drain-off supplies of petrol and oil for signalling purposes, check all available rations and water supplies. Try and repair any unserviceable or faulty equipment.

(g) *Institute Immediate Rationing.* No matter how much food and water you have, you should attempt to conserve it as long as possible by rationing. Do not cut the water ration below one pint per person per day unless in dire emergency. If food and water supplies from the aircraft are scanty, take immediate steps to implement them from natural sources. Don't leave it until you are too weak before you begin to hunt for your meals. If you can get food and water locally do so, and reserve your emergency rations for a real emergency.

(h) *Elect a Leader and Delegate Duties.* Normally the captain of aircraft will act as leader, but in special circumstances another member of the crew may be better suited. The captain may be injured, or one of his crew may be a jungle expert. In any event make a decision and stick to it. Each member of the crew should be given a special job, *e.g.* cooking, collecting water, building shelters, preparing signal gear, collecting edible plants, etc. Boredom and apathy can be dangerous to an idle man.

(j) *Relax and Formulate a Plan of Action.* After you have checked your equipment, don't be in too much of a hurry to start on "trek" towards the nearest town. There may be very good reasons for staying with the aircraft and there is plenty of time for careful thought. Assume from the start that you are in for several days in the jungle and another 24 hours either way will not make much difference. A good night's sleep in a well constructed jungle camp will make all the difference to a shaken crew. *Do not* relax if you have force-landed in enemy territory.

PLAN OF ACTION

15. If in wartime you have landed behind enemy lines, you must leave the scene of the crash at once. It may be advisable to split a large crew into parties of three or four men than to travel together. Once you are well clear of your crashed aircraft, set course for the nearest allied or neutral territory.

16. In peacetime or in friendly territory you must decide whether it is better to stay with the aircraft wreckage or to set out towards the nearest civilization. You may even decide to split the crew and leave some men with the aircraft while others go for help.

The main consideration is: *Are search aircraft likely to find you in less time than it will take to walk to civilization?* Once you start on "trek" there is little likelihood of your being seen from the air.

17. Once you have come to a decision based on careful consideration, put it into effect at once and stick to it. Your mental processes will be strained after several days in the jungle and you may later be tempted wrongly to abandon a good plan before it has had time to mature. Persevere and you will be successful.

18. Factors on which to base your decision are :—

(a) Do the authorities know that you have force-landed and do they know the position of the incident? If so, you will soon be found if you stay with the aircraft.

(b) If your position is not known, were you on track as per flight plan at the time of the crash? If you are missing, the first search will be along this track.

(c) Is the aircraft wreckage easily visible from the air? Can you make it visible?

(d) Have local forces sufficient aircraft at their disposal for an effective search; have the aircraft sufficient range to reach you?

(e) Is the weather favourable for search aircraft?

(f) Are transit or other aircraft likely to fly over your position? If so, how frequently?

(g) Do you know your own position accurately? If so, are you in easy reach of any known human habitation? Is the country between it and your present position easy to traverse? How long will the journey take you?

(h) Are all the crew fit for a journey through the jungle? Is any member so seriously injured as to need immediate medical aid? In the latter event, it may be advisable to send one party off for help while others stay with the injured man.

(j) Have you good supplies of survival equipment for a long march through the jungle : compasses, matches, etc.?

(k) What are your supplies of food and water? Consider the supplies available from aircraft emergency packs and those obtainable from natural sources. Is there a good water supply near your wrecked aircraft? Will you be able to live off the jungle when your emergency rations are expended?

(l) Lastly, how much do you know about jungle survival? If you have little confidence in your knowledge, stay where you are.

19. If you decide to remain with the aircraft you must ensure that every possible means of attracting attention is ready for instant use. Sound does not travel through thick jungle vegetation, so you can expect little warning of an approaching aircraft, and should one come within range the opportunity must not be lost. See that you are prepared and try to erect as many permanent indicators as you can.

    (a) *Permanent Ground Signals.* Parachute canopies spread out preferably over tree tops or in open clearings. Yellow dinghies inflated and placed in clearings. Bright panels or cowlings spread out near the aircraft, broken glass, the aerial kite flown above the tree tops, white clothing spread out on a line.

    (b) *Distress Signals.* Flame fires using petrol or dried wood by night; smoke fires, using oil or damp leaves by day; (keep fires lit all the time if the local wood is damp and fires are difficult to light); pyrotechnics; and fluorescence in streams.

20. If you intend to leave the aircraft you must first decide how much equipment to take with you. Don't take too much as you will soon find it heavy and cumbersome. Take such items as parachute canopies, for tents and hammocks; shroud lines for ropes, etc.; personal survival kits, first aid kits, fire axes and food and water. If you have not all got tropical back-packs a good container can be made from the parachute pack by cutting away surplus webbing. Another method of carrying equipment is to sling it on a long pole carried between the shoulders of two men. Don't discard too much clothing when setting out on "trek". The jungle is cold at night and you will need protective covering against mosquitoes and leeches, etc. Gloves are invaluable for clearing away thorns. When you leave the aircraft wreckage display a prominent notice saying where you have gone, and spread out the appropriate Ground Air Emergency signal.

JUNGLE HAZARDS

21. The large majority of people have an entirely erroneous impression of the risks and dangers involved in jungle travel. The majority think immediately of the big game, snakes, and other reptiles; so it must be made perfectly clear, that though the wild animals may abound in jungle country, they are as much concerned about keeping out of your way as, no doubt, you will be about keeping out of theirs. Where then are the dangers, from what source, and direction?

22. The greatest dangers lie in the demoralizing and cumulative effect of sometimes rather insignificant factors, which may be summarized under the following headings :—

    (a) Panic.

    (b) Sun and heat, and sickness therefrom.

    (c) Sickness, and fever—malaria, dysentery, sand-fly, typhus— are some of the more common.

    (d) Demoralizing effect and danger from all forms of animal life.

    (e) Poisoning, by eating or contact with plants. (See paras. 99 and 100.)

Most of these hazards are avoidable by taking precautions as provided by Service medical treatment, plus an elementary knowledge of personal hygiene.

Effects of Sun and Heat

23. The sun is highly dangerous because the effects are so frequently ignored. It causes sunstroke—or heatstroke—sunburn, and what is often referred to as heat exhaustion.

24. Sunstroke may occur at any time, day or night ; the victim becomes feeble and giddy, his throat is dry, he suffers from thirst, his skin becomes cold and clammy, the pulse increases and weakens, his temperature rises, he appears flushed, and he vomits. Move the victim into the shade, where there is a free circulation of air, strip to the waist and place in a sitting position on the ground. If possible spray cold water over the head and back, and give the victim ice or cold water ; as the temperature falls cover him with a blanket, and ensure he remains in the shade.

25. The prevention of sunburn is much easier than its treatment ; remember this when in the tropics. Many people become severely burned because they fail to realize that the effects of sunburn are not felt until too late ; that is, when you notice your skin turning pink, or feeling hot. When hazy or overcast, danger from sunburn is greater, as it is even less noticeable, there being so much reflected light. Should sunburn affect more than two-thirds of your body, it is likely to prove fatal. Therefore go carefully, take the precaution of keeping out of the sun as much as possible, and allow your skin to tan slowly, after which the dangers from sunburn are somewhat reduced.

26. Heat exhaustion is caused from long and continuous exposure to heat with high humidity, and may occur without direct exposure to the sun. The skin becomes cold and clammy with sub-normal temperature; the only cure is to get into the shade, and cover yourself to avoid becoming chilled, taking plenty of water and salt. Salt tablets should be taken daily if you have an ample supply of water available. Don't take them if water is scarce, as they will increase your thirst.

Sickness and Fever

27. *Malaria.* This is caused by the bite of an infected mosquito and the fever occurs at regular intervals after the first attack. As it begins the victim feels chilly and shivers; later in the attack he feels a burning fever. The hot and cold fevers alternate throughout the illness. Malaria may be prevented or minimized in two ways: by taking mepacrine consistently, and by avoiding mosquito bites. The latter course entails wearing long-sleeved coats and long trousers at all times. The jungle mosquito does not bite only by night, as the jungle is always protected from direct sunlight. The treatment for malaria is rest, copious drinks of water, and strong doses of mepacrine, six to eight tablets per day, until the attack is over. Once the temperature falls the patient can continue working or marching but there may be minor after-effects for some days.

28. *Dysentery.* Caused by eating or drinking polluted food or water. There are two types, but both have the same symptoms which are severe inflammation of the bowels and abdominal pains, and severe and continuous diarrhoea accompanied by green and bloody faeces. To prevent dysentery see that all doubtful food is cooked and all water purified. Be particularly careful near native villages where the vegetables, etc., are often fertilized with human excreta. To treat dysentery, sulphaguanadine is supplied in the tropical first-aid kit. Routine treatment is to put the patient on a soft liquid diet of milk, boiled rice, coconut milk, boiled bread, etc. The patient should take plenty of boiled water. Ordinary diarrhoea, which may be mistaken for dysentery, is often caused by stomach chills at night. To avoid chill, wrap a towel or cummer-bund around your stomach when you go to sleep no matter how hot you feel.

29. *Sandfly Fever.* Caused by the bite of the sandfly and has symptoms similar to malaria. To avoid the fever don't get bitten. Treatment as for malaria.

30. *Typhus*. Usually caused by the bite of an infected louse or a tick. The symptoms are a severe headache, weakness, fever and aching, the victim's face turns dusky, the tongue and lips become coated with a brown fur and on the fifth day the skin becomes

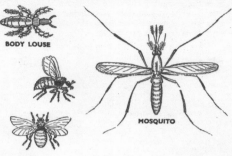

BODY LOUSE

MOSQUITO

SANDFLY

mottled and covered with a bright pink rash. Typhus is likely to prove fatal without medical attention. It can be avoided by regular innoculation and by personal cleanliness. Ensure that all ticks are removed from the skin and check clothes daily for lice ; wash the body at least once a day.

Danger from Forms of Animal Life

31. The forms of animal life differ in various parts of the world and a certain type might be dangerous to man in one part and not in another. The most deadly form of animal life is the mosquito which is found all over the world in different forms, but it can only be dangerous in certain areas.

32. *Mosquitoes*. The anopheles mosquito carries malaria and is a menace against which every precaution should be taken.

    (a) Always wear a mosquito net and leave no part of the body exposed.

    (b) If you have no mosquito net, a handkerchief, parachute canopy or large leaf can be used as a makeshift.

    (c) At night in particular, but at all times if possible, have trouser legs tucked into the tops of your socks, and shirt or tunic sleeves into gloves.

(d) When encamped, have at all times a smoky fire burning and sleep to leeward of it.

(e) Keep away from swampy and stagnant areas when resting or camping in the jungle, for these are the mosquitoes' breeding ground.

(f) There is no preventive innoculation against malaria, so very strict observance of these anti-malarial measures must be insisted upon at all times.

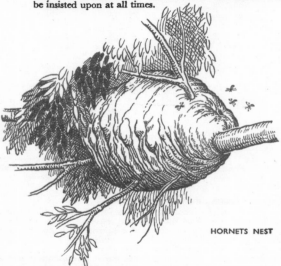

HORNETS NEST

33. *Wasps, Bees and Hornets.* These are dangerous pests. Their nests are generally brownish bags or oblong masses on trunks and branches at a height of 10-30 feet, and often on dead standing trunks. If a nest is disturbed and you are some yards away, sit still for five minutes and then crawl carefully away. Wasps go for moving targets, but should you be attacked, run through the bushiest undergrowth.

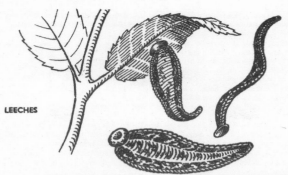

LEECHES

34. *Leeches*. Never pull them off, as their jaws will remain in the bite, and possibly fester and irritate. When moving through the jungle, if smoking, keep the pieces of unburnt tobacco, and wrap them up in a piece of material. When de-leeching, moisten the bag so formed, and squeeze the nicotine onto the leech. Other methods of de-leeching are the juice of the raw lime, salt, ash, and ash from a cigarette-end, or pipe. By using these methods, you force the leech to withdraw its jaws from the flesh and to drop off, with no risk of infection. Leave the blood clot on the leech bite as long as possible, squeezing it slightly at first to ensure the wound is clean, and the bleeding will stop in a few minutes. Leeches abound in lowland forest after rain, so keep a look out for these pests, and inspect your legs and boots every few minutes, and flick off any leech which has not yet got a hold. The large horse-leech will normally be found only in the sluggish lowland streams and swampy forest.

35. *Ticks*. Small grey ticks cause irritation, they swarm on plants or on dead fallen trunks, and might swarm onto a person in great numbers. Found during the wet season, ticks should immediately be removed from clothing, by hanging over or to lee-ward of a smoky fire; in the same way if ticks are on the body they can be smoked off. Remember also, when dealing with dead game, that ticks thrive on game, and especially on wild pig.

TICKS

36. Ants. The Red Ant makes its nest on the twigs of trees or shrubs, and is persistent in its biting attacks; other smaller biting ants have nests like earthy lumps, and it is wise to avoid trees with such apparent growths on them. Trees seen with leaves clumped together into small masses, or those on which ferns and orchids grow should also be avoided, as these will most probably harbour the biting ant.

ANTS

37. Snakes. Even the most deadly snakes prefer to glide away at the approach of man; but watch out for alarming one, or cornering it, particularly if following animal tracks, where they are found motionless on the ground, blending with their surroundings. Details of some of the snakes to be found in the jungle are given below :—

PYTHON

(a) *Python.* Length up to, but usually well below, 20 feet. A large constricting snake, sluggishly active by day and night. It prefers the forest, and may be found on the ground, up trees, or in the water. It is not of a timid nature, but though of very great strength, makes no attempt to avenge injury or offence. Has rarely been known to attack human beings.

(b) **_Hamadryad or King Cobra._** The largest of all poisonous snakes and is said to be the only one which will deliberately attack a man. It is olive or a yellowish brown in colour

KING COBRA

and may have a length of up to 18 feet. It is found in India, Malaya, South China and the Philippines. It is very aggressive and its bite is dangerous.

(c) **_Krait._** Length about 3 feet, colour glistening black with narrow white cross bars. It lives in fields, grass, paddy and low scrub jungle and is found in India, Malaya and South China. Its bite is lethal, but it will seldom attack even under provocation.

135

KRAIT

(d) **Banded Krait.** Colour black with broad yellow bands. Is found in the same countries as the ordinary krait, but prefers wet jungle areas. Not aggressive.

(e) **Cobra.** Length 5-6 feet. Its colour varies from pale brown to black. It has spectacle-like markings on the upper surface of the neck which are best seen when the hood is distended. It is most active by night, but will only attack man if disturbed or frightened. The bite is dangerous and may prove fatal in less than two hours. Found throughout Asia.

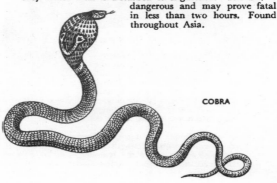

COBRA

RUSSELLS VIPER

(*f*) **Russells Viper or Tic-Polonga**. Length up to 4 feet, dark brown in colour with three longitudinal series of black rings. Its underside is normally white or pale yellow but is sometimes mottled brown, the head is large and ugly and is covered with symmetrical dark markings. It is nocturnal in habit, usually sluggish but violent when roused. It is particularly dangerous in that, because of sluggish nature, it fails to get out of the way, and when attacking it can jump its own length. Its bite may be fatal in 24 hours. Found throughout South East Asia.

(*g*) **Hump-nosed Viper**. Length about 30 inches. Its habits are similar to those of the Russells Viper, but its bite is seldom fatal. Generally found under dead leaves and undergrowth.

137

(h) **Saw-Scaled Viper.** Found in dry sandy areas where there is little vegetation. Its length is about 2 feet, and it is sandy yellow in colour with darker spots. It is aggressive and very poisonous. It may be found in the full blaze of the sun or beneath hot stones and in crannies heated by the sun. It has a habit of lying in a figure of eight with its head in the centre. Found in Syria, Persia and India.

SAW-SCALED VIPER

(j) **Sea Snakes.** Found around the tropical shores of the Pacific and Indian Oceans and in river estuaries. They do not frequent deep water. All sea snakes are poisonous but are seldom known to have attacked bathers. 2-4 feet long.

38. **Scorpions and Centipedes.** Although common in the tropics they are seldom seen in the open. They may be found under the

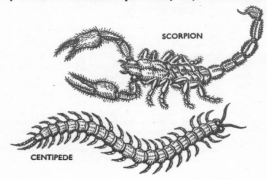

SCORPION

CENTIPEDE

bark of fallen tree trunks and under stones or rocks. Neither scorpion nor centipede will normally attack unless molested, but take care when handling rotten vegetation or when moving rocks. Inspect your boots before you put them on, as scorpions like to hide in discarded footwear.

39. *Sandflies.* Abundant by rivers, old forest clearings, and on sea shores. Take precautions as for mosquitoes.

40. *Big Game.* Most big game will avoid the scent and sound of man. If you travel noisily everything else will get out of your way. At night and in camp, keep a fire going to scare off wandering animals. Wild elephants may be inquisitive but will not approach a fire or light. Tigers are only dangerous when old and confirmed man-eaters. Avoid the banks of rivers, waterholes, and game trails by night and look out for crocodiles in the water at all times. Throwing stones is supposed to drive off crocodiles but you may not care to trust this.

JUNGLE TRAVEL

41. It is not generally possible to travel direct across country through the jungle. Your choice of paths will normally be restricted to streams and rivers, dry water courses, game trails, native paths, and along crests of ridges. These are the jungle highways and they have one thing in common—they run parallel to or follow the tilt of the land. Few jungle tracks cross from one valley to another or traverse a series of crests ; rather they run along the valleys or along the ridges separating the valleys. If there are no paths or streams, etc., and you have to cut across country, you may be able to make headway, but only at less than one mile per hour. Even a track 25° off your required bearing is better than no track at all. In jungle country you may find difficulty in reconciling the map and the compass. If in doubt, trust the compass, as jungle paths change position frequently and even rivers change their courses.

42. Tracks, game trails, streams, and ridges are animal highways at night, so keep clear of them in the hours of darkness.

43. To reach human habitation, follow down the course of a river or stream. Native villages are invariably sited on the banks and at the confluence of rivers which are the natives' trade routes.

44. If you wish to leave your camp site and later return to it, mark your trail. Blaze trees to show the white wood as you proceed, or cut off palm leaves and turn them upside-down to show their lighter undersides. Stones and broken branches will also mark a trail.

BLAZE TRAIL

45. If you are without a compass, follow a stream or river and do not attempt to strike across country. If you have a compass, use it constantly and maintain direction by sighting on a landmark ahead on your required bearing. Make for this landmark and then consult the compass again.

SPLIT ROOTS

46. If you wish to attract attention, do not wear yourself out by shouting. Hitting the trunk of a tall tree with a stout stick will make a drumming noise which carries much further than the voice.

47. In the lowlands trees with split roots will indicate swampy and perhaps tidal ground. Avoid all swamps, particularly mangrove swamps. The going is almost impossible and you are likely to get stuck half-way and have to turn back.

48. Never rush blindly forward. Whenever possible go slowly and deliberately, looking well ahead for hornets' nests, etc. Look out for snakes lying in the path. If you are in a party, travel in single file and have a "slasher" with a machete or knife in the van.

49. Do not tread or sit on rotten trunks or tree stumps, as they often harbour ticks. For the same reason avoid the wallows of large animals and wild pig. Never hit any dead or decaying vegetation without looking upwards. Dead branches may fall on you if you do not look.

50. In steep gullies or on hillsides there is often an accumulation of boulders and tree roots which become covered with mould and moss and form a false ground layer. Beware of breaking a leg by falling through this.

51. If you have no compass, you can judge direction by the sun, but you can only do so with accuracy in the morning and evening. At midday in the tropics the sun is so high that it is useless as a directional aid and you cannot find the North Point from your watch as you would do in England. Remember that the sun may be North or South at midday, depending on the time of year and your position relative to the equator. However, the sun always rises in the East and sets in the West. At night the Southern Cross gives a good indication of South.

52. For crossing streams and rivers make a raft of bamboo or some other light wood. Palm logs and jungle hard-woods do not float. If anyone has to swim across a river, throw stones in the stream and splash about to scare off crocodiles.

53. Take things easily, giving yourself a break every hour or thereabouts, depending on the type of country. This break of five or ten minutes should be utilized to discuss your route, take refreshment, to de-leech and to repair clothing and equipment. Make an early start and strike camp early so that by sundown the camp is organized and all are ready to settle for the night.

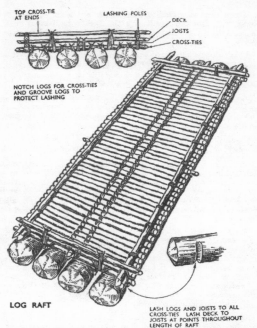

TOP CROSS-TIE AT ENDS

LASHING POLES

DECK

JOISTS

CROSS-TIES

NOTCH LOGS FOR CROSS-TIES AND GROOVE LOGS TO PROTECT LASHING

LOG RAFT

LASH LOGS AND JOISTS TO ALL CROSS-TIES. LASH DECK TO JOISTS AT POINTS THROUGHOUT LENGTH OF RAFT

54. Take all normal precautions to keep yourself fit and see that other members of the party do the same. Scratches and bites should be attended to right away, and make sure that due care and attention is given to the feet. This involves taking off all footwear at night and, where possible, washing and drying socks and stockings. Check footwear in the morning for scorpions by tapping them on the ground. If you find you are getting blisters on your feet, stop at once and put a dressing over the blister. Do not wait until the blister becomes unbearable.

CAMPING SITES

55. The requirements of an ideal camp site are as follows :—
    (a) Proximity to water and food.
    (b) Solid ground free from mud.
    (c) Freedom from dead and decaying vegetation and insects.
    (d) Freedom from overhanging branches, or from coconuts overhead.
    (e) Natural protection from weather and animal life.
    (f) Concealment in wartime.

56. Unless one is able to keep dry and free from insects and other irritants, there will be little rest during nights spent in the jungle : so take some care over the selection of the camp site. Make your decision in good time so that the site may be made safe and comfortable before nightfall. Do not, however, insist on finding a place which meets all the above requirements or you are likely to search all night.

57. Start off by clearing away all dead and rotting vegetation, as such rubbish encourages ticks, ants, leeches, etc., and as soon as possible light a fire, as the smoke will drive away those irritating insects, quite apart from being ready to cook and heat water later on, as required. Arrange for a supply of bamboo, if it is available, as it will be found invaluable for cooking and boiling water.

PALM BED AND SHELTER

CAMPING SITE

58. Make yourself a bed, either by utilizing the parachute canopy you have brought with you or by collecting twigs and small branches from the trees, covering a cleared area of ground with them, and then adding a further covering of leaves. This will ensure your having a good night's rest, and also insulation against ground chill and dampness. You are likely to be very cold at night, so don't discard blankets and heavy clothes if you have them with you.

59. Your fire will produce a certain amount of ash, which should be removed from the fire, and spread in an unbroken line around the camp site, thus ensuring no intrusion from the innumerable insects to be found crawling around on the floor of the jungle.

DON'T camp in river beds, though they might look clear and dry, as a storm in the hills might flood the river in a few hours.

DON'T be too concerned about the proximity of water. If making camp for an indefinite period, consider the laying-on of a water supply by using sections of split bamboo in the form of guttering, having tapped the stream at a point further up from the camp site.

DON'T overlook the necessity of making sanitary arrangements, as this will avoid risk of developing one of the numerous diseases affecting the intestines. See that all refuse is deposited well clear of the camp, and buried if possible. (See First Aid and Personal Hygiene.)

FIRES

60. On the assumption that you have the means to kindle a fire, the following points should be borne in mind :—

(a) Use judgment in the selection of a fire site. Pick a spot where there is no danger of the fire spreading ; dry and sheltered if possible. During the wet season find a dry spot under a leaning tree or similar shelter.

(b) Use dry fuel, which may consist of dry grasses or plant stems, dry leaves or bark from trees. Dead wood from trees, and pieces found in rotting trunks or fallen branches will be found to be dry even in the wet season. Do not use wet bamboo as it may explode in the fire and throw out dangerous splinters.

(c) Have a good supply of firewood and kindling available before starting a fire, and having got some of the smaller pieces of wood to burn, add the others and build the fire up, rather than attempt to start with a large one.

61. A fire, quite apart from giving a little moral comfort, discourages the approach of any wild animal, and also smokes away all forms of insect life. Remember when leaving camp to ensure that the fire has been properly extinguished, either by watering thoroughly, or spreading the ashes and stamping them out. In

dry country, prone to forest fires, use both methods and travel on with a clear conscience.

Methods of Kindling

62. Although one reads of various methods of kindling a fire, apart from using matches, most of these will be found rather unsatisfactory. Rubbing pieces of wood together, or producing a spark from two stones or flints is all very well, but in practice it will not produce results in the hands of the inexperienced. It is, however, most essential for the "jungle hiker" to conserve his waterproof matches, as, rather obviously, these are going to be the easiest means of producing fire.

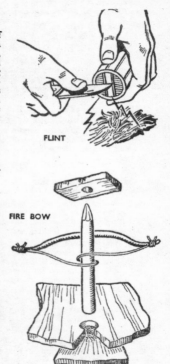

FLINT

FIRE BOW

63. Another satisfactory way is by using a piece of magnifying glass, or lens; often termed a "sun-glass". Aircrew flying over desolate tropical country should always see that they have one amongst the various "odds and ends" they choose to carry with them.

64. If faced with the necessity of producing flame without matches first of all see that you have everything ready to start a fire, such as plenty of dry small wood and kindling, and choose a suitable spot. Then go in search of a piece of straight dry wood, well seasoned; such wood might be found amongst dead trees;

pick a soft wood in preference to a hard wood, and use one of the following methods :—

(a) *Fire, with Bow and Drill (see illustration)*. Draw the bow backwards and forwards, causing the drill to spin in its hole, the action should be slow full strokes at the beginning, and working up to a fast stroke as the smoke begins to rise. Once smoke has been seen to come from the hole in the block a spark should be found large enough to start a fire. Take the block, and add a little tinder, blowing gently—you should then get a flame ; but be sure to build up the fire from a small start, otherwise it will most likely be smothered, and go out, when the whole procedure will have to be done again.

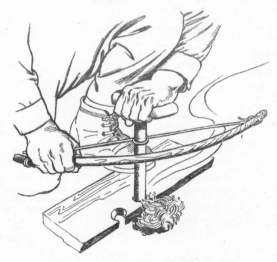

BOW AND DRILL METHOD OF MAKING FIRE

(b) *Fire Thong.* Obtain a length of dry rattan, and draw it smartly across a soft dry piece of wood. Have the kindling underneath, ready to catch the embers as they drop.

(c) *The Fire-Saw.* This is another simple method, but requiring rather more physical strength and stamina than the other methods. It is just a question of drawing one piece of wood across another. A piece of split bamboo or soft wood will serve as one piece, using a sawing motion across another section of wood.

RUBBING TWO PIECES
OF WOOD TOGETHER

Methods of Cooking

65. Food is generally more palatable and safer to eat when cooked than when eaten in its raw state, and there is no reason why anyone stranded in tropical country shouldn't have a hot cooked meal. Probably the most simple method is by "broiling" over a fire ; all that is required is the fire and some means of supporting the food. This method can be used to great advantage with fish, and small joints, or animals.

66. Yams, potatoes, and some other roots can be placed immediately in the fire, and left until they feel tender. Clean, and remove the skin, and the meal is ready for serving.

67. The gipsy method of cooking certain types of meat is another simple, yet very effective, method. This involves the collection of mud, or clay ; the food to be cooked is covered with it and placed in the fire. When ready remove from the fire and when the clay is broken open, the food will be found clean, and ready to eat. In the case of the porcupine, this method also removes all his quills with the greatest of ease.

68. Boiling food is always a good stand-by, and it is generally a question of finding a container in which to boil the water. This should not cause any difficulty, particularly if in the vicinity of a jungle stream or river, as a selection of bamboo will, no doubt, be found along its banks. There are two simple methods of boiling with the aid of bamboo, which incidentally will last for only two or three meals, before the wood becomes charred and leaks. If a considerable quantity of water is required, take a length of bamboo, perforate each water-tight section, except the bottom one, suspend over the fire, using a forked stick, in the manner of the illustration.

69. If only a small quantity of water is required to boil some fruits or vegetables, etc., take one section of bamboo, cut a hole in the top, and suspend over the fire by means of two horizontal sticks, or two pieces of jungle vine or rattan.

BOILING WATER

70. If bamboo is not available make a vessel from fibrous barks or leaves. A container thus made will not burn below the water-line ; moisten the area above the water-line to reduce the risk of the

149

container burning from the top. Keep the fire small, and the flames low, and there should be little difficulty in producing the required results.

Suggested Methods of Cooking various Types of Wild Food

71. *Fruits.* Boil succulent fruits, and bake or roast the thick-skinned and tougher variety.

72. *Potherbs (vegetables).* These are best boiled. In some cases, it may be necessary to boil in two or three changes of water in order to remove undesirable acids, etc.

73. *Roots.* Either bake, roast, or boil; the former is probably the easiest of the three methods in this case.

74. *Small Game.* These may be cooked whole or in part; if uncertain as to the quality of the meat, boil first, then roast or broil.

75. *Fish.* All methods of cooking are suitable for fish meat, and remember that most of the fresh water fishes should be boiled, before eating or cooking by any other method.

76. *Reptiles.* The smaller varieties can be toasted over a fire, but such things as snakes, eels, and turtles are best boiled. In the case of the latter, when cooked the shell will come away from the meat; it makes a good meal if boiled in vegetables, with the meat cut up. Serve as a stew or soup.

77. *Crustaceans.* The simplest method of cooking these is by boiling. They require little cooking, but will spoil very quickly after being caught.

SALT

78. This is required in cooking, and to ensure the proper functioning of the human body. It can be obtained from sea water, also the ashes of burned nipa palm boughs, hickory, and one or two other plants contain salt that can be dissolved out in water. The salt remaining after evaporation is a dark gritty substance. The salt tablets from the Tropical First Aid outfit can be used for cooking.

WATER

79. Survival is more dependent on a supply of drinking water than on any other factor. Your emergency rations are no good to you unless you have the drinking water to go with them. Remember that with water alone one can expect to survive for about three weeks, but without water the average man will last no longer than two to five days.

80. In tropical forest, the availability of water is not so great a problem as its purity, and the table given later in this section shows where water can be obtained, and which of the sources should be purified before drinking. All non-flowing water found on the surface should be purified, and there are a number of alternative methods of doing this, as shown :—

(a) Use the halazone tablets in the Survival Kits, and allow to stand for 10-15 minutes.

(b) Use two or three drops of iodine to one quart of water, and allow to stand for 30 minutes.

(c) A few grains of permanganate of potash to one quart of water, and allow to stand for 30 minutes.

(d) Make a container from bamboo, if nothing else is available, and boil for at least three minutes.

RAIN TRAP

81. Numerous jungle plants have natural receptacles in which water will be found ; though in certain cases, such as the cups of the pitcher plants, the water will be foul with decaying insects and quite impossible to drink. One of your most plentiful sources of water is in the jungle vines, or the rattans, which hang suspended amongst the trees and jungle vegetation. By cutting a length of about four feet, from the lower portion of the vine, the jungle

hiker will obtain a quantity of cool refreshing water, in no need of purification. A word of warning, however; look out for those vines giving a milky or dark-coloured sap, as they should be avoided.

82. When drinking from a jungle stream, if you consider the water pure and fit for drinking, don't drink direct from the surface, but cup your hands, or use a drinking mug of some sort, so that you can see what you are drinking, and avoid swallowing such things as leeches, or other small water life. If you find a plentiful water supply, drink as much as you can, as the body can store plenty of water for future use.

83. At times, it is often found necessary to use for cooking and drinking, water obtained from animal watering places, or large rivers, the water being muddy, and cloudy. This is not necessarily dangerous, and this water can be purified by one of the methods mentioned above. It is better to filter this water, and endeavour to clear it ; this can be done by allowing it to stand for a while, overnight perhaps, with a cover on the container. Then, to filter, use a sand-filled cloth, or a bamboo stem, filled with leaves or grass.

84. *Sources of Water in Tropical Forests.* Fresh water, not in need of purification :—

   (*a*) *Rain.* Build a rain trap from large leaves, with framework made up from bamboo or branches.

   (*b*) *Jungle Vines (and Rattans).* Select the lower loop of any vine, and cut out a length of four or five feet, from which drinkable water may be drained.

   (*c*) *Streams.* All fast flowing streams, having a mixed sandy and stone bed, provide clean water. If there is no sign of animal deposits, or sewage within half-a-mile up stream, this water will also be pure, and ready for drinking.

   (*d*) *Plants.* During the monsoon or rainy season water can be collected from natural receptacles found on various plants. This will be fresh rain water, and fit for human consumption.

   (*e*) *Bamboo.* In the base of large bamboo stems will be found drinking water. It is not possible to guarantee finding water from this source on every occasion.

   (*f*) *Coconuts.* In the green unripe coconut will be found a very good substitute for fresh water, *i.e.* "coconut milk". One nut may contain as much as two pints of this delicious cold fluid. Do not drink the "milk" from the ripe, or fallen coconuts.

85. Sources of Water which should be Purified before Drinking

(a) *Water Holes.* Water found here will probably be muddy, and with pieces of rotten vegetation in it, so filter it first, then allow to stand for a few hours, filter again, then purify by one of the methods suggested at para. 8o.

(b) *Digging.* Treat water as for (a) above. If on the seashore, dig a small hole a few yards above high tide, and as soon as you find water collecting, stop digging. Water collected in this way should be fairly free from salt, the fresh water floating on the top of salt water, hence don't go too deep. The water obtained in this way may taste slightly brackish, but will be safe to drink. If very strong, filter it a few times, or try again further up the fore-shore.

(c) *Stagnant Water.* This is not necessarily infected, but in order to make sure, filter it, then purify. Stagnant water may be found in small pools, amongst rocks, dead tree-stumps, etc.

(d) *Large Rivers.* This water will be muddy and probably infected, so treat as for water holes.

SOLID FOOD

86. Plant food alone is not likely to keep you alive indefinitely unless you are prepared to spend all day hunting for it. It will, however, prove a welcome addition to other food and will keep starvation away for several days. There are a number of potential food plants to be found throughout the jungle, but the most common, found in abundance in the tropics, are mentioned here. These are selected because of their abundance, simplicity of preparation for eating, and comparative ease with which they can be recognized.

87. In addition, it is to be strongly recommended to those stationed in tropical areas that they obtain the assistance of a native guide, and arrange for an instructional walk through a typical part of that country over which they operate, or visit the nearest botanical gardens.

88. There is no need to worry unduly about the effects of poisonous plants, for though a few might be considered highly dangerous, the greater number will most likely cause you to be indisposed for a matter of days. With reasonable care, and by taking the normal precautions when taking strange foods, your troubles should be small. Should you at any time be uncertain of the plant you wish to try, the following points may be of guidance :—

(a) Eat sparingly of any strange plant, until you can be quite certain as to the reaction, if any, it might have on you.

(b) Avoid all those things which are unpleasant to the taste, those which are bitter, or acid, etc.

(c) Avoid those plants, with one or two special exceptions, which give a milky or soapy sap.

(d) If in doubt, endeavour to see what the monkey thinks of the food, for you can always rely on him deciding whether plants are fit to eat.

Selected Foods

89. *Sweet Potatoes.* Have a vine-like growth, with leaves, and flowers that resemble those of the "morning glory". The potatoes

SWEET POTATO

may be eaten raw or cooked, the latter by placing in a ground oven, or in the base of a fire after which clean them, and peel. In addition to the potato, the young shoots and leaves are delicious when boiled, and make an excellent substitute for spinach.

90. **Taro.** A plant two or three feet in length, with a large heart-shaped leaf, resembling "elephant ears". Taro has thick potato-

TARO

like roots which differ in size, according to variety. This plant provides one of the natives' staple foods. The roots and young leaves and stalks are all edible, but must be cooked, by boiling or roasting, which are generally the simplest of methods. After cooking, the roots may be peeled, then mashed into a doughy-like mass, with the addition of a little water. This may be preserved, if required, for a few days, by wrapping in leaves.

91. **Tapioca.** Known as cassava or manioc. The plant is shrubby and three to seven feet high, with large tuberous roots, this being the edible portion, which vary in size from six inches to

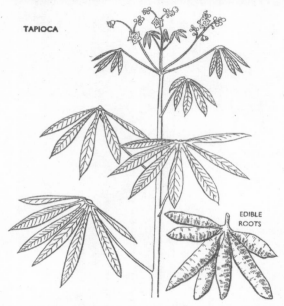

TAPIOCA

EDIBLE
ROOTS

as much as two feet. There are two basic types, the sweet type, and the bitter : and one can only be distinguished from the other by the taste. Avoid the bitter type, unless it can be cooked, as it is highly poisonous, containing the basis of the deadly hydrocyanic acid. To cook the bitter type, grate or mash the roots into pulp, squeeze out the juice, and make the remaining "dough" into cakes, which can then be baked in the ordinary way.

92. *Breadfruit.* Should always be cooked before eating. The most practical way is to bake the entire fruit in hot embers for

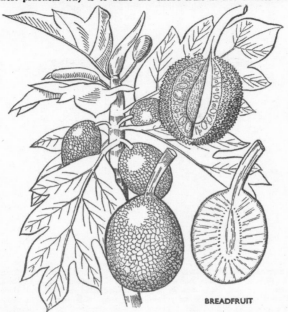

BREADFRUIT

half-an-hour or so, then peel off the skin before serving. It can also be boiled, baked, or cut into slices and fried. To preserve, boil first, then cut into strips, and allow to dry-out in the sun. When required these slices can be served without any further preparation. The seeds may also be eaten if boiled or roasted.

93. **Ferns.** Several varieties are abundant in many areas, and are to be found in marshes, swamps, along water courses, and

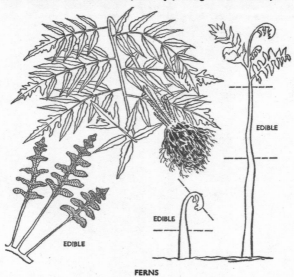

FERNS

other camp shady places. The tree ferns will be found throughout the forests. The tips and shoots of most of the ferns are good food, raw or cooked, and because of their widespread distribution, their accessibility, and ease of recognition, may well serve as a most important source of diet. Ferns, like all the food to be found in the jungle, should be taken in small quantities during the first few days, as the change in the form of diet may have an adverse effect on the stomach and intestines and cause diarrhoea. Though ferns are so readily available, they are not particularly nourishing, and if other forms of food can be found, it would be well to vary the diet.

94. *Bamboo*. Here is a good emergency food, which is familiar to everyone, and is widely distributed throughout all tropical

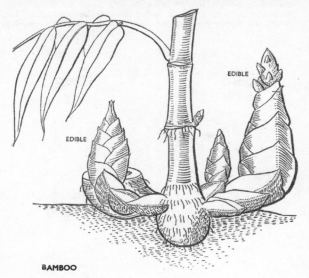

EDIBLE

EDIBLE

BAMBOO

climates. The young shoots, up to a foot or so in height, can be eaten raw, but are more palatable if cooked. See that the fine black hairs along the edges of the leaves of the small shoot are removed before cooking, as they are poisonous.

95. *Coconuts*. These contain, not only good drink, but also good food. First there is the meat inside the nut itself, which makes good eating, and also can be made to yield coconut oil, which is a useful preventative for sunburn. In addition there is the palm "cabbage". The cabbage is found in the top of the palm, inside the sheath from which the leaves protrude, and may be eaten raw, boiled, or roasted. Where it tastes pleasant it makes an excellent vegetable though some varieties may be bitter. The coconut is an excellent food and palm trees are numerous, but getting the nuts is not quite so easy; healthy coconuts do not fall

COCONUTS

off trees, but have to be plucked by hand. If you can get a native to go up the tree, so much the better; if not pick a small and sloping tree and climb up as best you can. When you have got the coconut, the next problem is to open it. The husk may be cut away with a machete, but the best way is to place a stout

BREAKING COCONUTS

pointed stick in the ground point uppermost and bang down the coconut on the spike. When you have got a split in the husk, use the spike as a lever to prize it off; once the husk is removed it is easy to break open the inner shell.

96. *Seaweeds.* All forms of seaweed are edible; oddly enough they are not particularly salty in flavour, and their water content is fairly fresh. Seaweed is probably more palatable in its raw state, and the best types will be found amongst the pink and purple variety and the reddish or green types.

97. *Water Lilies.* Those types found on the surface of fresh-water lakes and in streams are a source of food. All these types

WATER LILIES

are edible, and the seeds and thickened roots of all varieties may be eaten boiled or roasted.

98. *Fruits.* It is amongst the infinite number of different fruits to be found in the tropics that the main troubles lie. There are quite a number of poisonous types, and it would be well to receive some local advice as to those types found in abundance, which are either edible or poisonous. Fruit found in native allotments is safe to eat.

Poisonous Plants

99. In order to avoid the poisonous plants to be found throughout the tropics, and in particular the Far East, the following rules should be observed and the list of poisonous plants identified and memorized :—

  (a) Do not eat red—or brightly coloured—fruits and berries unless you know them to be harmless. Avoid anything looking like a tomato, though it might smell quite pleasant.

  (b) Do not eat roots, fruits, and vegetables with a bitter, stinging, or otherwise disagreeable taste. If in doubt, taste with the tip of your tongue, or take a minute piece spitting it out immediately should you consider it to be amongst the poisonous variety.

  (c) Avoid all contact with any plant, shrub, or tree, with a milky sap.

  (d) On certain types of young bamboo there is a prickly form of down, which causes intense irritation and sores. When working this type of bamboo, be certain to wear your jungle gloves, or at least cover your hands.

  (e) Leave all toadstools or mushrooms alone.

  (f) Because birds and animals eat certain types of plants, it is no guarantee that it will be safe for human consumption, as most animals can digest foods that are poisonous to man. In an emergency, if you can find nothing eatable, watch the food the monkey eats, as you can be certain that he is eating food fit for human consumption.

100. *List of Poisonous Plants.* A few of the most common and more dangerous of the poisonous plants are listed separately as follows:—

Grows wild throughout the tropics. Seeds contain deadly strychnine.

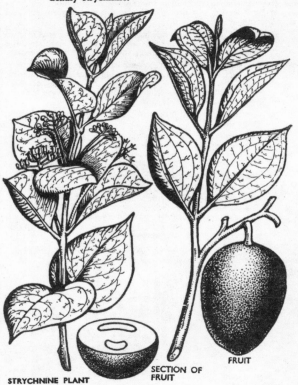

STRYCHNINE PLANT

SECTION OF FRUIT

FRUIT

(b) ***Milky Mangrove, or Blind-your-eyes.***
Found in mangrove swamps, on coast or estuaries.
Sap causes blistering, blindness if in the eyes.

SEEDS   FLOWERS

MILKY MANGROVE OR BLIND-YOUR-EYES

(c) *Cowhage, or Cowitch.*
   Found in thickets, and scrub. Not in true forest.
   Hairs on flowers, and pods, cause irritation and blindness
   if in the eyes.

COWHAGE OR COWITCH

FRUITS

(d) Nettle Tree.

Widespread, especially in and near ponds. Poisonous to touch, causing burning sensation. Relieve with wood ashes, moistened.

STINGING HAIRS

NETTLE TREE

FLOWER

(e) *Thorn Apple.*

Common weed of waste and cultivated land. All parts, especially the seeds, are poisonous.

SEED

SEED POD

THORN APPLE

(f) **Pangi.**
Found mainly in Malayan forests. Seeds of the large brown fruits contain prussic acid.

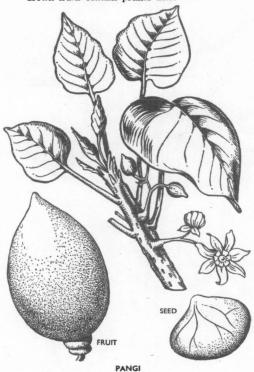

SEED

FRUIT

PANGI

(g) *Physic Nut.*
Common in fences, and hedgerows. Large seeds, violently purgative.

PHYSIC NUT

SECTION OF FRUIT

(h) *Castor Oil Bean.*

A shrub-like plant common in thickets and open sites. Seeds are poisonous, and a violent purgative.

CAPSULE

FEMALE
FLOWER

MALE
FLOWER

SEEDS

CASTOR OIL BEAN

(j) *Rengas Tree*

Widespread in Malayan forests. Localized rash caused from contact with bark, timber, or water off the tree.

RENGAS TREE

SEED

FLOWER

101. *Birds*. All birds are edible, though a few, including the carrion-eating vultures and kites, have a flesh which is most unpleasant to the taste.

102. *Lizards and Snakes*. All these are edible, the meat from the hind quarters and tail in the case of the lizard being the best. Snakes are not going to be so easy to catch, or to find for that matter, but if you do happen to contemplate a meal of snake, remove the head immediately the reptile has been killed. Frogs are quite good food but they should be skinned before cooking.

103. *Ants, Grubs, etc.* Natives consider the white ant as a delicacy, either cooked or raw, with the wings removed. Also the white grubs of wood-infesting beetles are edible, and will be found quite palatable, if split and broiled over a fire. They will be found in decaying and rotten wood. Such insects as grasshoppers and crickets may be toasted over a fire, the wings and legs having first been removed.

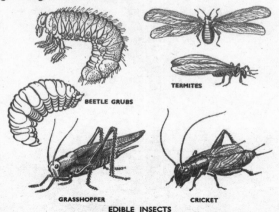

TERMITES

BEETLE GRUBS

GRASSHOPPER

CRICKET

EDIBLE INSECTS

104. *Animals*. Too much reliance should not be placed on animals as a source of food. They are not only difficult to catch,

but finding them in the first place may present quite a problem, and killing them and disposing of the flesh will also need considerable thought. Those animals most easily found and caught are probably the various species of deer and wild pig but you will need a gun to kill them. A bow and arrow will kill small birds and animals; you can catch others in traps.

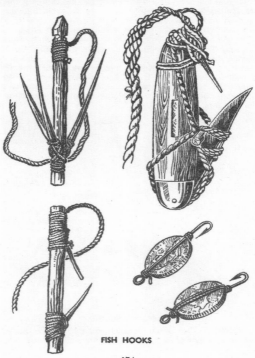

FISH HOOKS

FISH HOOKS

Fish

105. All areas of water, lakes, streams, and rivers contain a variety of life, most of which will be found to be edible. If camping in the vicinity of water there should be no danger of shortage of either food or water—fresh or purified— all of which can be obtained from such a source. Animal life is more abundant in water than on land, and generally speaking, is more easily caught. The chances of survival along a body of water are always excellent, and fish may be caught with crude equipment, if you know when, where, and how to fish.

106. *When to Fish.* Different species of fish feed at all times of the day or night, though there are many governing factors relating to feeding activity; however, in general, early morning and later afternoon are the best times to fish with bait. Fish rising or jumping are sure signs of feeding.

107. *Bait.* Experiment with bait, and try to obtain your baits from the water, as such bait will be more natural. Such life as insects,

shrimps, worms grubs, small minnows, or even the meat of a jellyfish, are all good bait ; in addition the wasted parts of the fish themselves, that is the eyes, head, intestines. If a certain type of fish appears plentiful, having caught the first one, open it up and find out on what it feeds, and endeavour to find a similar bait.

108. *Technique.* Try to conceal the hook in the bait, and approach the fish upstream, as they normally lie heading into the current. In clear shallow water, move slowly to avoid frightening, and if unsuccessful, try fishing after dark.

109. *Hooks and Lines.* Hooks can be made from pins, needles, wire, or any pieces of available metal ; fishing gear can also be made from wood, bamboo, bones, large thorns, or a combination of these ; see illustrations. Lines can be made from a great variety of plants, or the wiry stems of high climbing ferns, and the inner bark of trees, or the skin of the banana tree-trunk. For added strength a number of these can be twisted or platted together.

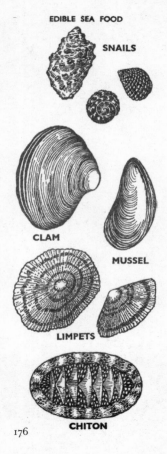

EDIBLE SEA FOOD

SNAILS

CLAM

MUSSEL

LIMPETS

CHITON

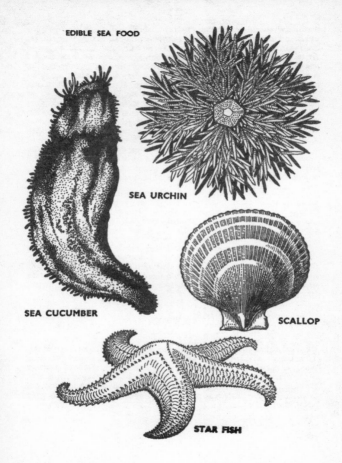

EDIBLE SEA FOOD

SEA URCHIN

SEA CUCUMBER

SCALLOP

STAR FISH

110. *Crustaceans.* Crabs, crayfish, lobsters, shrimps, and prawns are found in fresh water throughout the world; all of them are edible, though they will spoil quickly. As is the case for all types of fresh water fish, the crustaceans contain parasites harmful to man, and must always be cooked before serving. Many species are nocturnal in their habits, and may be caught more easily at night. All the meat within the skeleton of crabs, crayfish, and lobsters can be eaten, but the gills are usually discarded. Fresh water shrimps are abundant in tropical streams, and can be seen swimming or found standing stationary on the rocks and the sand of the stream bed. Look for them in the quieter parts of a stream where the water is sluggish. They can be caught quite easily with a small cane, with a loop at the end made from the skin or bark of a tree. The idea is to drop the loop over the eye of the shrimp, which protrudes from its head, and with a quick movement the shrimp is caught in the loop. They will rise to the surface at night, if a light is placed close to the surface, and may be scooped off.

111. *Fish Traps.* A simple and very useful fish trap, capable of catching all types of creatures found in fresh and salt water, can be made from two pieces of bamboo. The scheme is to obtain one small piece about a foot in length, and another rather larger and somewhat longer piece, perhaps about two feet. Split each piece down from the top, leaving the bottom intact, force the ends out to form a cone, and then place one cone inside the other, attaching the edges together with cord, or some fine flexible vine or rattan. A hole made in the smaller cone will turn this device into a simple "lobster pot", and two or three of these placed in the stream near to the camp will produce meals without time or effort being spent. (see illustration to para 127).

NATIVES

112. In peacetime you can expect natives to be friendly. In troubled areas you will be briefed of possible hostility before flight. The natives will, no doubt, know of your presence however quietly you may approach. If uncertain of your reception, send one member of the party into the village first. Whilst he is away, move to another position ; in the event of antagonism, it will be possible to get away before the natives appreciate that you have moved from your point of observation.

113. Having made contact, if receiving shelter or hospitality from

natives, throughout the time you are with them consider the following points :—

(a) Deal with chief, or headman, and ask, do NOT demand.

(b) Show friendliness, courtesy, and patience—don't be scared, as fear tends to make them hostile.

(c) Do not threaten or display weapons.

(d) Greet natives as you would your own kind.

(e) Make gifts of small personal belongings and trinkets.

(f) Take plenty of time when approaching either them, or their village.

(g) Make use of the sign language; when ready state your business briefly, and frankly.

(h) Treat natives like human beings, and don't "look down" on them ; after all, you will be wanting their help sooner or later.

(j) If you make a promise be sure to keep it.

(k) Respect local customs and manners.

(l) Endeavour to pay in some manner for what you take ; using tobacco, salt, razor blades, matches, cloth, empty containers, etc.

(m) LEAVE THE NATIVE WOMEN ALONE—only have contact with them when on "official business".

(n) Respect their privacy, do not enter their homes until asked.

(o) Learn their laws, and abide by them—bounds, animals, etc.

(p) Entertain and be a good audience.

(q) Take practical jokes in good fun.

(r) Try to pick up bits of their language ; they will appreciate your efforts, when you make use of some of their words.

(s) Avoid all leading questions—with the answer "yes" or "no".

(t) Learn their woodcraft, and the sources from which they obtain food and drink.

(u) If living amongst natives, endeavour to avoid personal contact with them as much as possible ; make your own shelter, and produce and cook your own food and drink.

(v) Always be friendly, firm, patient and, above all, honest.

(w) When you depart be sure to leave a good impression.

SURVIVAL EQUIPMENT

114. Survival equipment is available in two forms, namely emergency packs which are carried in larger aircraft, and personal survival kit. This equipment should be carried on every flight, and frequent checks should be made to ensure that it is intact and in good condition. Every item is invaluable and it is imperative that you should know how to use the equipment to the maximum advantage before the emergency arises.

PERSONAL HYGIENE AND FIRST AID

115. It is most important for the "jungle hiker" to appreciate the necessity of taking every precaution against disease and infection, caused from lack of care and attention. One of the most important, though not the most obvious—so it seems from past experience—is the care of the feet.

116. *Care of the Feet.* Since a hiker will not get very far if his feet let him down, all hikers must take care of the feet. This involves the discarding of all footwear at the end of the day, the washing and rinsing of socks or stockings, leech stockings—if used—and jungle boots, etc., and also the feet. Allow footwear to dry by the camp fire overnight, and replace the following morning. Try to prevent foot-rot, as once it develops it is most difficult to eradicate.

117. *Camp Sanitary Arrangements.* All camp sanitary arrangements and refuse pits, etc., must be well clear of the camp. When any waste is deposited, a layer of earth should be thrown in to cover it, and thus avoid infection.

118. *Water.* Take great care to see that precautions as suggested in paras. 79-83 are enforced. Try to avoid camping too close to your water supply, and when collecting water, or washing, etc.,

in the vicinity of a stream or watercourse, do NOT hang around in a half clad state, but get away from the midges, mosquitoes, and other irritating forms of insect life, as soon as possible. See that members of the party wash at least once a day, paying due care to anti-malarial precautions, etc.

119. *Bites.* If leeches and ticks are removed by one of the recognized methods (see para. 34) there should be no danger. The small amount of bleeding after the leech has released its hold ensures the wound being clean. If in doubt apply some antiseptic. This also applies to ticks, methods for the removal of which will be found in para. 35. Untreated bites may develop into jungle sores.

120. *Snakes.*

(a) Though the danger from snake-bites is considerable, it is by no means as great as one is led to believe. Untreated snake-bites, even that of a cobra, are not always fatal ; though this will depend to some extent on the health of the victim, and that of the snake ; and upon whether the snake has exhausted its poison or not, in the process of feeding ; the poison being a digestive agent. Death, from a snake-bite, may be caused either from the snake venom, or from shock and fear. In dealing with such a bite, it is necessary to act swiftly—seconds count—but KEEP CALM.

(b) Treatment of a snake-bite aims at preventing the absorption of the poison into the system, and the reduction of the poison from a possible fatal dose to a non-fatal dose.

(c) Make a lengthwise cut through the bite, and as deep as the bite, with additional shallow cut near the wound. Cut parallel to blood vessels and tendons, don't cut indiscriminately.

(d) Suck out the blood and venom, if your mouth and lips are free from cuts and sores, otherwise force out by squeezing.

(e) If a limb has been bitten, place a tourniquet above the wound, *i.e.* between wound and heart, but take care to avoid stopping the blood flow from the heart to the wound, as the bleeding will assist in removing the poison. To do this, tighten the tourniquet until the pulse stops, then loosen so the pulse is just felt. If the wound is in the lower part of the arm or leg, use a tourniquet above the joint, and another above the wound, massaging the limb towards the wound to encourage the blood flow. Loosen tourniquet every 15 to 20 minutes.

(f) Keep the victim quiet, and avoid any movement or exercise, stimulant and/or alcohol. A cold wet cloth applied in the vicinity of the wound will tend to delay the absorption of the venom.

(g) Kill the snake, if possible, as this will help considerably in identification ; an important point if serum is available.

(h) Do not cauterize, or use potassium permanganate, as this destroys the tissues, and does more harm than good.

NOTE. The above instructions also apply to bites from most poisonous insects and reptiles, except that as few of these are ever likely to prove fatal, the application of a tourniquet may not be necessary.

121. *Blisters.* Remove all pressure from a blister ; by cutting away shoes and improvizing footwear from parachute packs and canopy, or plant leaves and fibres, in the case of the feet. If the cause is due to equipment carried, improve on the carrying arrangements, and if too weighty, consider slinging on a bearer, carried by two members of the party. Avoid breaking a blister, but prick the edge with a sterilized instrument—hold in flame or boiling water—and press out the fluid. Keep the blister clean and dry, using bandages improvized from parachutes, clothing, etc., and don't overlook any disinfectant that is available. If blisters should continue to give trouble, the best way of avoiding complications is simply to stand fast for a day or two. Bathing one's feet in very hot salt water is most comforting, and also hardens the skin. See para. 116 for "Care of the Feet".

122. *Rashes.* Those caused from contact with various forms of poisonous plant can frequently be relieved by the application of some oil and bandaging. If no oil is available, coconut oil can quite easily be obtained from the nuts, or apply some wood ash, moistened in water, as a paste, which will be found quite soothing. Prickly-heat and foot-rot are both caused from poor personal hygiene, and if suffering to any extent with either it is best to rest for a few days, to allow the skin to heal. To acclimatize the skin against prickly-heat and sunburn acquire a good tan as soon as you can. When you are working hard or walking fast wear your shirt outside your trousers to allow air to circulate close to the skin.

123. *Insects—General.* There is available a very effective insect repellent, and when travelling through the jungle make good use of it. A band about an inch wide, placed around the upper part of the jungle boot, or on the trouser-leg, or stocking, will discourage the advance of leeches, both during the "hike" and particularly during "stand-easy". If using the parachute hammock, soak an inch or two of the shroud lines in the repellent, and you will not be worried by insects, which might attempt to approach along such a "line of communication".

JUNGLE CRAFT

124. The ability to provide yourself with shelter, camping equipment and food, will increase your chances of survival, and at the same time, reduce your own physical hardships. One of the most useful and most common sources of material for jungle-craft is the bamboo. This will be found in abundance along streams or rivers which you may be using as a means of communication or transport, and with the aid of a good jungle knife, and a little imagination, can be turned into all manner of useful articles. A word of warning to those who start working bamboo ; be careful of the hard and extremely sharp outer skin, which will split up, and may very easily cause a deep and subsequently dangerous wound.

125. Though bamboo may seem rather difficult to work to the inexperienced, after two or three days the art will develop, when its uses in camp and the daily jungle routine will be found inexhaustible. Not only can the stems be used, but the leaves, if laid over a framework to form a roof, will be found durable and weatherproof.

126. Apart from watching out for cuts from the outer skin, the only points to remember in working are the methods of cutting. First, if cutting through the stem, make the cut at about 45°-50°, when it will be found quite simple to make a clean cut, without splitting. Sometimes it may be necessary to cut longitudinally, such as when making table-tops, or fish traps (see para. 111) in which case lay the bamboo on firm ground, and cut into it with a strong easy stroke, rolling the bamboo, and thus working round its circumference.

127. Some of the more common forms of equipment improvized with the aid of bamboo are listed and illustrated :—

(a) Simple lean-to shelter, or more complex hut or bungalow.

(b) Furniture, such as chairs, tables, beds, etc.

(c) Household tools, and hunting weapons, harpoons, etc.

(d) Cooking and boiling or stewing pots, and drinking mugs.

(e) "Clappers" for use as sound signalling apparatus.

(f) Traps, for catching fish, and all forms of wild animal, large or small.

(g) Rafts, and barges, for transporting personnel and equipment.

(h) Finally, bamboo may be burnt as fuel, if broken up and left in the sun to dry, and the shoots are quite a delicacy as food.

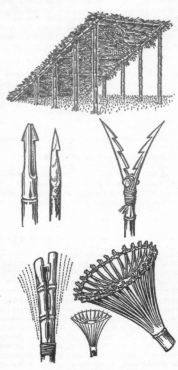

BAMBOO IMPLEMENTS

128. A question that is often asked is: "We know it is quite possible to make a great number of useful implements from bamboo, and other plants, but they all require a lot of cord, or rope. How are we going to make do, unless we have a regular and continuous supply of such material?" This is a very important point, but one that is soon put right, as there are inexhaustible supplies of plants from which cord, lines and rope can be made. A list of these is given below:—

- (a) *Breadfruit.* Strands of inner bark.

- (b) *Plantain and Bananas.* Fibrous tissues and mature leaf stalk, and strands from the outer covering of the trunk of the banana tree, will make good fishing line.

- (c) *Coconut Palm.* Fibres of coconut husks, and midrib of leaves.

- (d) *Liana.* Smaller stems, and the fibres of larger ones.

- (e) *High Climbing Ferns.* Wiry stems are very durable under water.

- (f) *Climbing Canes.* Stems.

- (g) *All Vines and Rattans.* Smaller flexible stems, or stem fibres.

- (h) *Tropical Weeds.* Fibre from inner bark.

- (j) *Wild Hibiscus.* Stem fibres.

- (k) *Screw Pine.* Leaf fibres.

JUNGLE SURVIVAL TRAINING

129. *Practical Experience and Familiarization.* The first and most important step in survival training is to look at some jungle. If you are stationed in the Far East there is likely to be some jungle within reach. If, however, you are in a well developed part of the country, the local areas of forest reserve will provide what you want. Even a ten minutes' stroll along a jungle path will enable you to appreciate the problem of survival and movement. Squadron and station rescue officers should organize short trips through the jungle with a local guide who can point out edible and poisonous plants. This training should be developed until air crew are capable of making cross country journeys from point to point through jungle with the aid of a compass. If jungle hiking alone becomes boring, hunting and shooting excursions will add interest and perhaps reward to the training.

130. *Plant and Animal Familiarization.* Most towns in the Far East have their own botanical gardens; the large cities have museums and sometimes zoos. The curators of these institutions will be only too pleased to help you identify the plants in their collection and will point out poisonous snakes, etc. Station rescue officers should maintain a regular programme of visits to such places.

131. *Jungle Craft.* Survival training on the station should include practical work in Jungle Craft. Aircrew should practise fire lighting (without paper), making animal traps, fishing, shelter building, raft making, and use of bamboo, etc. One can also usefully practise the art of opening coconuts.

CONCLUSIONS

132. The jungle is by no means as formidable a place as the average person imagines. There are many difficulties and snags ; but the large majority of these can be surmounted, and eventually, with due care, consideration, and perseverance, one can expect to arrive amongst friends. Undoubtedly a little weary, worn, unkempt, and certainly sick of jungle foods, hard rations, and the irritating forms of jungle life ; but nevertheless, safe and sound, ready to carry on as before.

6/50   E41191/43544   Wt.35484-BN.3785   (T.S. 30014)   4,250   3/53   Gp. 8
Fosh & Cross Ltd., London

Ground/Air Emergency Code for Use In Air/Land Rescue Search

KEY

1 REQUIRE DOCTOR, SERIOUS INJURIES
2 REQUIRE MEDICAL SUPPLIES
3 UNABLE TO PROCEED
4 REQUIRE FOOD AND WATER
5 REQUIRE FIREARMS AND AMMUNITION
6 REQUIRE MAP AND COMPASS
7 REQUIRE SIGNAL LAMP WITH BATTERY, & RADIO
8 INDICATE DIRECTION TO PROCEED
9 AM PROCEEDING IN THIS DIRECTION

10 WILL ATTEMPT TAKE-OFF
11 AIRCRAFT SERIOUSLY DAMAGED
12 PROBABLY SAFE TO LAND HERE
13 REQUIRE FUEL AND OIL
14 ALL WELL
15 NO
16 YES
17 NOT UNDERSTOOD
18 REQUIRE ENGINEER

CODE

1	I
2	II
3	X
4	F
5	≫
6	□
7	– • –
8	K
9	←
10	I>
11	⌐
12	△
13	L
14	LL
15	Z
16	Y
17	JL
18	W

* A SPACE OF 10FT BETWEEN ELEMENTS WHEREVER POSSIBLE

SEA

SURVIVAL

AIR MINISTRY PAMPHLET 224

SEA SURVIVAL

INTRODUCTION

1. Survival at sea for days, perhaps weeks, in difficult conditions, is a possibility facing all aircrew who fly over the sea. The fate of a crew is usually settled in the first few hours after ditching, and survival depends on two vitally important factors :—

   (a) *Morale.* This is the first essential to survival in any circumstances ; without it no amount of material aid will suffice. Morale is made up of will-power and determination to live, good crew discipline, and good leadership.

   (b) *Knowledge.* A thorough knowledge is required of :—

      (i) Emergency drills. These should be practised for all possible contingencies until they become instinctive.

      (ii) The principles of survival and the use of emergency equipment.

      (iii) Emergency signals procedures.

      (iv) Search and rescue organization.

   If possible, the salient points of emergency drills and survival should be covered in the pre-flight briefing, especially when passengers are being carried.

DITCHING, DINGHY, PARACHUTE, AND SWIMMING DRILLS

2. It is not within the scope of this pamphlet to discuss emergency drills in detail (A.M. Pamphlet 212, " Emergency Drills ", deals fully with this subject) ; in fact, it is assumed that a safe alighting has been made in the sea by ditching or by parachute. However, knowledge of emergency drills is such a vital link in all survival, that, for the guidance of all captains of aircraft and crew members, a number of important points and often fatal mistakes are included below.

3. *Ditching and Dinghy Drills*. Ditching and dinghy drills are carefully calculated, and are not hit-or-miss affairs. Drills vary with aircraft, but the following points should always be considered :—

    (a) Number and size of exits.

    (b) Number of crew.

    (c) Type and stowage of dinghies and emergency equipment.

    (d) Previous information gained from model or actual ditchings.

Experience has shown that most multi-engined aircraft break up aft of the main spar, so crews should be placed forward if possible. Wireless operators' and navigators' ditching positions should be near their place of work, since they are working up to the last minute. Rear gunners should not be left in their turrets.

4. *Dangers Attendant upon Ditching*. Dangers can be summarized under three headings :—

    (a) Injury on impact.

    (b) Failure to escape.

    (c) Failure to survive.

5. *Injury on Impact*. Providing the pilot can execute a reasonable ditching no one need suffer any injury. Injuries are usually caused by the person failing to brace correctly, or through not knowing his drill. Injury may also result from loose or incorrect stowage, or inadequately stressed equipment within the aircraft fuselage. Therefore :—

    (a) Know how to brace. You can withstand 10*g*, or even more, if correctly braced.

    (b) Know your ditching stations.

    (c) Stay braced until the aircraft stops. Wait for the second impact as the nose hits the water.

6. *Failure to Escape*. Purely the fault of bad dinghy drill, such as :—

    (a) No exits open.

    (b) All trying to get out at once.

    (c) Pilot has left bomb doors open.

    (d) A lower hatch is not locked and the aircraft sinks quickly.

7. ***Failure to Survive.*** The initial causes are :—

   (a) Faulty drill.
   (b) Faulty signals procedure.
   (c) Failure to understand the emergency.

At the first sign of trouble the captain must initiate the correct difficulty, emergency, or distress procedure ; the more information the controller receives the more efficient is his search.

8. ***Personal Precautions.*** If possible, do not ditch wearing a collar or tie. Make sure that your life-saving waistcoat is serviceable and inflate it with one breath only. Inflation may not be advisable, however, in aircraft with small exits.

9. ***Ditching Positions.***

   (a) Facing aft, back braced against bulkhead in a seated crouched position, knees bent and hands clasped behind the neck to prevent neck injury.

   (b) In certain aircraft where seats are near emergency hatches it may be advisable to remain in the seat, relying on the stressing of the harness to afford protection. If facing forward, the head should be cradled for protection in the arms or in a seat cushion against a suitable support, such as a table. Rear facing seats are the best. Violent decelerations should be guarded against.

   (c) If neither of the above positions is practicable, the deceleration may be guarded against by lying braced transversely across the fuselage floor, or flat on the floor facing forward with feet braced against a support with the knees bent.

   (d) One man is always to be in inter-communication with the pilot.

10. ***Parachute Drills.*** These are laid down for each aircraft to enable crews to clear aircraft quickly and efficiently, and are based on :—

   (a) The shortest and quickest means of getting to escape hatches.
   (b) The even distribution in the use of escape hatches.
   (c) The best sequence for personnel in using hatches.
   (d) The best method of jumping to clear internal and external obstructions.
   (e) The height from which the escape is to be made.

11. *Swimming*.

  (a) Don't discard your clothing.
  (b) Swim slowly and steadily ; in any case your progress will
      be limited when wearing a life-saving waistcoat.
  (c) If you must swim through fire, jump feet first, upwind of the
      aircraft. Swim into the wind using the breaststroke, and
      try to make breathing holes by splashing the flames away
      from your head and arms. You may be able to swim
      under water, after first deflating your life-saving waistcoat.
  (d) If there is a danger of under-water explosions while you
      are in the water, the likelihood of injury will be reduced
      if you swim or float on your back.

12. *Final Hints.* In conclusion, stay with the aircraft and do
not bale out, unless there is structural failure, uncontrollable fire,
or the ditching characteristics of the aircraft are so poor as to make
an attempted ditching extremely hazardous. If a ditching is
inevitable and you have sufficient warning, it should be carried out
while some use of power remains. Even when " K " type dinghies
are carried, the advantages of a successful ditching are that the
crew will be together, in a larger and more seaworthy dinghy ;
they will be less exposed, with more equipment, and will be more
easily seen from the air. In consequence, their morale and their
chance of survival should be much greater.

IMMEDIATE ACTIONS AFTER DITCHING

13. Immediately after a ditching, certain actions have to be carried
out. These must be drilled until they become instinctive, and yet
they must be flexible enough to cover such contingencies as injury
or death of any member of the crew, which would necessitate one
man doing the work of two in the precious seconds before the aircraft
sinks. These immediate and subsequent actions are detailed in
paras. 14 to 18.

14. *Release and Board the Dinghy.* Inflate the dinghies and
get aboard, as laid down in the drill. Don't jump in or you may
damage the dinghy. Don't board an inverted dinghy, for if the air
beneath is expelled a suction is created and the dingy may be
difficult to right (see Fig. 1). Make sure that all the survival equipment goes aboard, especially a parachute pack, which is probably
the most valuable single piece of survival equipment. With a little
ingenuity it can be made to serve a multitude of purposes, especially
in the clothing line.

15. **Roll Call.** The captain of each dinghy calls the roll, endeavours to find any missing crew or passengers, and then cuts the painter. Thus it can be seen that in a passenger-carrying aircraft the complement of each dinghy should be clearly defined before take-off.

16. **Paddle Clear and Salvage Equipment.** Paddle clear of the aircraft. Beware of any jagged metal. Beware of the aircraft as it sinks, especially the tail plane. Salvage all floating equipment and lash all equipment securely to the dinghy. One of the occupants should then securely attach himself to the dinghy with a length of line—a safety precaution against losing the dinghy through it overturning and drifting away.

17. **Stream Sea Drogues and Service Dinghy.** Rendezvous with the other dinghy if more than one has been launched and secure the dinghies together. About twenty-five feet of line between dinghies has been found to be the best length to avoid snatching.

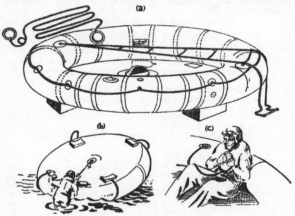

(a)

(b)   (c)

Fig. I.   TYPE "J" DINGHY

(a) Type "J" Dinghy   (b) Method of righting dinghy   (c) Topping-up

Stream the sea drogues to minimize dinghy drift. If necessary, top-up the buoyancy chamber using the topping-up bellows. Bale out with the baler and Viscose sponge. The sponge, which resembles a flat biscuit, will need plenty of soaking before it reaches its full size. If the sea is rough, rig the weather aprons to keep the occupants and the inside of the dinghy dry.

18. *Administer First Aid.* First aid should be administered without delay to the injured and to those suffering from shock. Injured personnel usually require extra water, food, and clothing, a point to be borne in mind when rationing. Wet clothes should be removed and dried, if you have spare clothing. In very cold weather, put on your protective clothing immediately if you are not already wearing it, otherwise you will be forced to keep on your wet clothing rather than risk exposure. That parachute silk will now come in handy for making improvised shirts, socks, and leggings, secured with pieces of shroud line. See paras. 26 to 28 for precautions against weather and details of dinghy ailments and first aid treatments.

PLAN OF ACTION IN DINGHY

19. When the immediate actions after ditching have been completed, the captain should discuss a plan of action with the crew. If the captain is missing or badly injured it will be necessary to appoint another captain before trying to formulate the plan of action. Apart from easing the general tension, the discussion should serve to obtain the full agreement of the crew on all points of the plan. The points enumerated in para. 20 should be considered.

20. *Factors Affecting the Plan of Action.*

   (a) The state of W/T contact and the amount of information signalled before ditching.
   (b) The likelihood of air search and its probable efficiency in the prevailing weather.
   (c) The position of ditching in relation to the nearest land, surface craft, main shipping lanes, and air routes.
   (d) Knowledge of, and the advantage to be gained from, wind, current, and tides. This will be important in the tropics where air search may be limited in scope, and it may ultimately be decided to make a landfall.
   (e) Rations available, particularly water.

21. The decision must then be made on whether to remain in the vicinity of the ditching or to set course for an area where help is

more likely. Generally, it is preferable to remain in the vicinity of the ditching for at least 72 hours ; but should circumstances favour a departure from this area (*e.g.* proximity of land, shipping lanes, etc.) no time should be lost in getting " under way " so as to take advantage of the crew's initial fitness and energy. The plan of action should be adhered to, despite any temptation to change it later, for it was formulated when all were in a state of mind to think and plan coherently.

22. *Dinghy Log.* A log should be kept throughout the period in the dinghy. The first entry should include all details of the emergency : the names of survivors; date, time, and position of ditching; the behaviour of the aircraft at ditching and the length of time it remained afloat; weather conditions; items of equipment salvaged; and details of available rations. Later entries should include details of the dinghy's progress, notes on crew morale and physical condition, rations issued, weather, and aircraft sighted.

23. *Signalling Gear.* All signalling gear should be checked and prepared for instant use, according to the instructions supplied with each item. The following hints should enable you to make your signals more effective and help to conserve them.

(a) The life of the battery in " Walter " varies from about 20 hours continuous running in temperate conditions to 8 hours in tropical or arctic conditions. To conserve the battery, switch on the transmitter for periods of only 2 minutes at intervals of 5 minutes, except when an aircraft is heard or sighted, when it should be left on. When the aircraft has sighted and marked the dinghy's position and is homing a rescue surface craft, switch the transmitter on and off for 20-second periods.

(b) The Dinghy Radio S.C.R. 578 is your only W/T link, so transmit as long as your strength will allow, but you must transmit at the hour plus 10 to 20 minutes and 40 to 50 minutes. These periods will cover the listening watches of search aircraft, ships, and shore stations.

(c) Hold on to pyrotechnics until an aircraft is seen or heard, and do not expend them until certain of results. Aircraft searching for you at night will, weather permitting, fly between 3,000 and 5,000 feet, and will fire a single green pyrotechnic at intervals of 5 to 10 minutes depending on the ground speed and visibility. When you see the pyrotechnic fired by the aircraft, allow 30 seconds to elapse, then fire a red pyrotechnic, followed by a second one after a short interval. This second pyrotechnic enables the aircraft to check the alteration of course made towards you. Additional pyrotechnics need be fired only if the aircraft appears to be getting off course, and finally when it is almost overhead.

(*d*) Make sure all the crew can use the heliograph. When the sun is shining this is your best visual signalling device, and on a bright day the flash can be seen for 15 miles. The dinghy radio signal lamp can be used at night for automatic or manually keyed visual signals.

(*e*) Try to conserve your fluorescene sea marker. Although once it has been in the water it is supposed to be useless for a second time, it is not necessarily so. The main problem is to prevent it contaminating your food and water when it is brought aboard after having been wetted. To make the best use of the fluorescene marker, the following is suggested. If your W/T or R/T contact before ditching was good and your distress signals were acknowledged, allow sufficient time to elapse for search aircraft to reach the area, then stream the fluorescene block and leave it out. If your W/T or R/T contact before ditching was poor, stream the block only if an aircraft is seen or heard and bring it in again if you are not located.

(*f*) Remember that aircrew whistles can be used to help a man in the water to locate the dinghy, or in an attempt to attract the attention of passing surface craft.

ALLOCATION OF DUTIES

24. Duties should be allotted by the captain to all occupants of the dinghy. This will help to prevent those mental disturbances, indicated perhaps by outbursts of temper over trivial matters, which are likely to arise as a result of apprehension and exhaustion. In any case, these duties will be invaluable to your plan of survival.
25. Duties should include signaller, navigator, aircraft spotter, and fisherman, and in a large crew can be rotated by means of a watch system. A record of duties carried out should be entered in the log, which is kept by the captain and his second-in-command. The duty of distributing the rations is the sole responsibility of the captain, the issues being recorded in the log to avoid arguments.

PRECAUTIONS AGAINST WEATHER

26. *Hot Climates.* In hot climates some form of sun shelter should be erected in the dinghy, care being taken to avoid any restriction of air round the occupants. Unnecessary clothing should be discarded, but the whole body should remain covered with one thin layer of material. The head and neck should always be kept covered. During the day, clothing should be worn soaked in sea-water, but it should be dried out thoroughly before sundown. Eyes should be protected from sunlight and reflected glare by wearing sun glasses or improvised eye shields. As a precaution against sunburn, which can occur even in cloudy weather, the anti-sunburn cream from the first aid packs should be used. Mild exercise, involving slow and easy movements of the limbs, should be taken, but over exertion should be avoided. Every precaution should be observed against sunstroke and heat exhaustion.

27. *Cold Climates.* In cold climates it is essential to keep oneself and the inside of the dinghy as dry as possible. All wet clothing should be removed and dried, if dry clothing is available; otherwise dampness should be reduced as far as possible by squeezing the wet clothing. A wind break should be rigged, and loose articles of clothing or a parachute wrapped round the body. There should also be adequate insulation against the cold floor of the dinghy. So that body heat may be transmitted to persons suffering from cold, occupants should lie together in the bottom of the dinghy. Hands can be warmed under arm-pits, between thighs, etc. Mild exercise should be taken to prevent stiffness of muscles and joints, and face muscles should be exercised frequently to ward off frost-bite.

PROTECTION OF HEALTH

28. The ailments likely to be suffered by survivors at sea are chiefly caused by exposure to weather and sea-water, and by shortage of fresh water.

(a) *Seasickness.* The performance of duties requiring some concentration helps to ward off seasickness. Its treatment is to refrain from eating and drinking for some time, to lie still, and to maintain bodily warmth. Anti-seasickness tablets are provided in the larger first aid kits.

(b) *Immersion Foot.* Exposure of legs and feet to cold water for some time results in damage to the tissues. The affected part becomes red and painful and difficult to move. This is followed by swelling, the appearance of blisters and dark patches, and breaks in the skin. Prevention lies in keeping the feet as warm and dry as possible, and in ensuring that the floor of the dinghy is dry. The toes and feet should be moved frequently to assist blood circulation, and tightly fitting boots should be discarded. Remedial action is to remove footwear ; wrap feet in loose, dry articles of clothing or strips of parachute ; raise the feet clear of any water ; and keep the body warm. The affected parts should not be rubbed. " Everhot " bags should on no account to placed near the affected limb ; they may, however, be used to maintain bodily warmth.

(c) *Salt Water Sores.* These are boils or " burns " caused by exposure to salt water. Prevention is by keeping the body as dry as possible. The sores should be cleaned but not squeezed, and sulphanilamide crystals should be applied. Large sores should be covered with a dressing.

(d) *Sore Eyes.* Sore eyes result from excessive exposure to glare from the sky and water, and should be treated with boracic ointment and bandaged lightly. In the absence of a suitable ointment, a damp bandage should be applied.

(e) *Parched Lips and Cracked Skin.* These discomforts may be remedied by the application of any greasy ointment, such as boracic or vaseline.

(f) *Constipation or Difficult Urination.* These complaints should not give cause for alarm, as they are to be expected with a shortage of food and fresh water.

(g) *Frost-Bite.* The symptoms of frost-bite consist of small patches of white or cream coloured skin, stiff and firm to the touch. A prickling sensation may be felt. If the condition is allowed to become serious, tissues and bone may become frozen and blood-cells clot. When the affected part is warmed, there will be a swelling and redness of the skin with accompanying pain depending on the degree of frost-bite. Frost-bite is usually experienced in extreme cold ; exposed fingers, nose, and ears being most susceptible. Protection is obtained by keeping as warm and dry as possible, moving limbs, and exercising face muscles. Affected parts must not be rubbed or massaged, but warmed gently with breath, warm hands, or other warm parts of the body. The precautions to be observed against the direct heat of " Everhot " bags are the same as for immersion foot.

DANGEROUS FISH

29. Dangerous fish, such as the shark, barracuda, and swordfish, are most common in tropical waters. Without provocation, they will not normally attack you or the dinghy. However, a brief description of these fish, together with a few simple hints, should help to safeguard you from attack or injury.

30. *Sharks.* Ocean sharks have the power to kill, but in the tropics, where their food is abundant, they are not normally ferocious. They are cowards and can usually be frightened off by the jab of a stick, a blow struck with the fist or a knife, particularly at the nose, or by the splash of water. Making a commotion in the water, however, may attract sharks from a distance. The tiger shark can be identified by the black stripes on its dorsal fin and sides ; natives do not regard it as more savage than other sharks. Reef and lagoon sharks are much smaller, ranging up to only four or five feet long. They are considered harmless by the natives, but they may snap at you if they are allowed to come too close. The only shark of which the Polynesians are really afraid is the *niuhi*, or man-eating shark, which will sometimes attack without provocation (Fig. 2). Fortunately it lives in deep water and rarely comes to the surface. It can be identified by its dark blue dorsal fin and back, and its stubby tail. The tails of other sharks have a long upper lobe.

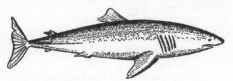

Fig. 2. MAN-EATING SHARK

31. *Barracuda.* The barracuda is aggressive and is similar in appearance to a pike, except that it has two large dorsal fins in line on its back. Its rather elongated body and long pointed jaws should help you to recognize it.

32. *Swordfish.* There are many varieties of large fish, similar to the swordfish, all possessing a long bill or sword with which they attack shoals of small fish for food. They are not normally dangerous unless attacked or wounded, when they have been known to ram a boat (Fig. 3).

Fig. 3. SWORDFISH

33. *Wading Dangers.* If putting ashore or wading in search of food, especially in the tropics, be careful where you put your hands and feet. Apart from wounds which may be inflicted by coral, there is always the danger from eels such as the Moray eel, sting-rays, and poisonous shellfish (Figs. 4 and 7). See also paras. 52 to 54 on poisonous fish.

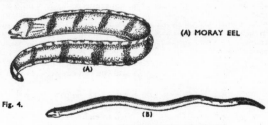

(A) MORAY EEL

Fig. 4.

(B)

(B) POISONOUS SEA SNAKE

34. *Hints on Dealing with Dangerous Fish.*

    (*a*) Keep clothing on and keep a good look out.

    (*b*) Do not fish if sharks, barracuda, or swordfish are in the vicinity.

(c) Do not trail hands or feet over the side of the dinghy.

(d) Do not throw waste food or scraps overboard during the daytime.

(e) If dangerous fish are about, remain quiet, and the likelihood of attack will be negligible.

(f) Survivors in the water without a dinghy should form a circle facing outwards and beat the water with strong regular strokes, if sharks are about.

DRINKING WATER

35. Drinking water is your most essential need. A man in good health can live from 20 to 30 days without food ; without water he can live only for about 10 days, and even less in the tropics. A man needs a minimum of a pint (20 ounces) a day to keep fit, but he can survive on two to eight ounces a day. Therefore *the rationing of water must be instituted without delay and not relaxed until final rescue.*

36. *Water Rationing.* The sources of water in your emergency packs and survival kits are made up of sea water de-salting apparatus, and tins, bottles, or cushions containing fresh water. A still may also be included. The de-salting apparatus and still should be used first, while you still have the mental ability and patience to cope with them. A plastic drinking cup is provided, marked in nine divisions of approximately two ounces each, and should be used for rationing. While no hard and fast rules can be laid down for the rationing of water, the following method is recommended :—

(a) *1st Day.* No water issued, except for the injured. The body acts as a reservoir and you can live off the water it has stored.

(b) *2nd, 3rd, and 4th Days.* 14 ounces per head daily, if available.

(c) *5th Day Onwards.* Two to eight ounces per head daily, depending on the climate and the water available. Rain water, and water obtained from any additional source, must also be rationed, except while it is raining as explained in para. 38

37. When drinking, the lips, mouth, and throat should be moistened before swallowing.

38. *Rain Water.* For survival over a prolonged period, especially in the tropics, you will be dependent on rain for your drinking water. You must always be prepared to improvise a rain trap with the dinghy weather apron, at the first sign of rain. The salt should be washed off the apron with the first rain water collected, and then all possible containers should be filled. At the same time, drink your fill slowly and deeply. Don't drink quickly after being on short rations, or you may vomit.

39. *Icebergs.* Icebergs are a potential source of drinking water in polar latitudes, but extreme caution should be exercised in approaching them. In the lower latitudes icebergs are usually well eroded and should be avoided, as they are liable to overturn without warning. The flat-topped icebergs and the small " growlers " of the higher latitudes are safe to approach.

40. *Old Sea Ice.* Sea ice is of two main types. Young sea ice is salty, like the water from which it was formed, but after a year it loses its salt and becomes almost fresh. Old sea ice can be distinguished by its smooth rounded corners and bluish colour. Young sea ice is rougher and milky-grey in colour. In summer, drinking water can be obtained from pools in the old sea ice or from melting brash ice floating in the vicinity.

41. *Immersion of the Body.* It is possible to reduce your thirst by immersion of the body in the sea, although you must remain in the water for an hour or more to gain any real benefit. Immersion will be most beneficial in the tropics—if sharks are not present. Above latitude 50 deg., the coldness of the water is likely to do more harm than good.

42. *Fish Juices.* Experiments have been made to squeeze the juice from fish and use it as a water substitute, but without any great success. It has also been advocated that fish could be cut into cubes and chewed for the moisture content. General opinion, however, is no longer in favour of these methods, as it is considered that additional fresh water would be necessary to assimilate the protein in the fish juices. Furthermore, it would require a fish of about 20 pounds to produce a pint of juice.

WATER RULES

43. To preserve the water in the body is almost as important as having water to drink, so here are a few very important rules for guidance :—

(a) **Keep your shirt on,** in every sense, to prevent the loss of body moisture through unnecessary perspiration and exposure. Rig up some sort of awning, but not so as to restrict the cooling effect of the breeze. When the sun gets up, keep the clothing wet with sea water, the evaporation of which will cool the body, but discontinue if chilliness results. Rinse accumulations of salt from the clothing so that the skin will not be harmed. In the later afternoon, allow the clothing to dry ready for the night.

(b) **Sleep and rest** are most important during a shortage of water. In the tropics, keep your exercise to a minimum. The body relies on the evaporation of sweat to keep its temperature constant and, if you keep moving around, it is possible to lose up to two quarts of body moisture in a day.

(c) **Prevent seasickness if possible.** Valuable water can be lost through being sick. Seasickness tablets are contained in the larger dinghy first aid outfits, and should be taken at the first feeling of sickness.

(d) **Do not drink sea water,** or attempt to make your fresh water last longer by adding sea water to it. It will only increase your thirst and make you violently sick.

(e) **Do not drink urine.** It is injurious and will only decrease your resistance and increase your thirst.

(f) **Do not drink alcohol.** It will nauseate you and increase your thirst by drawing water from the intestines and kidneys, and may give you convulsions. Alcohol has no thirst-quenching value and is dangerous to drink in these circumstances.

(g) **Keep smoking to a minimum.** Smoking increases thirst, and smokers should be encouraged to cut it out or to reserve smoking for the night watches, when they will find it more soothing and less likely to make them thirsty.

(h) **To allay thirst,** and keep the mouth moist by increasing saliva, it may be found beneficial to suck on a piece of cloth or a button. Chewing gum may help, but it sometimes has the effect of increasing thirst.

(j) *Do not eat unless you have adequate water for digestion.* Water and food in survival are closely related. In the following section on food, it is explained that the amount of drinking water available determines the type and quantity of food which may be eaten.

FOOD

44. In the adverse conditions of survival at sea, it is vital to realize that the amount of the water ration will determine how much food may be eaten and of what it should consist, for the body requires water for the digestion of food and the elimination of waste products. Food can be divided into two main categories, so far as the balance between food and water is concerned. These are :—

(a) *Carbohydrate foods, i.e.* sugars and starches, which require very little water. Represented by potatoes, fruits, and the food tablets and sweets in the emergency flying rations.

(b) *Protein foods,* which require a large amount of water. Represented by meat, fish, shellfish, eggs, and certain green leaf vegetables including seaweed.

45. *Food and Water Rules.* As far as the survivor at sea or the castaway is concerned, it is sufficient to follow three simple rules :—

(a) The quantity of the food and water rations must be varied in direct proportion to each other. If you have plenty of water you can increase the food ration, but as the water ration decreases the food ration must also be decreased.

(b) Protein food, such as any raw fish, bird, or seaweed, will require more water than your emergency flying rations.

(c) Live off natural foods if your ration of water will permit, and save your emergency flying rations for the real emergency when your water supply is getting low.

Emergency Flying Rations

46. There are two types of ration, each containing carbohydrate foods, and therefore invaluable for sustaining you when your water ration is low. The Type " P " ration contains peanut toffee ; the Mark 3 contains malted milk tablets, barley sugar, chewing gum, and energy tablets. Each personal survival kit should contain one of each of these, and the aircraft's emergency pack should contain one Mark 3 ration per man.

47.   No hard and fast rule for rationing can be given, but a minimum of four malted milk tablets or their equivalent in peanut toffee per day is sufficient to sustain life. The barley sugar can be used occasionally to relieve the monotony of this diet. At this minimum ration, one tin of rations will last one man approximately 12 days and your rationing scheme can therefore be planned accordingly.

Fish

48.   Fish represent your largest possible source of natural food and the great majority of fish are edible. In the tropics, a rough and ready rule is that the fish of the open sea, out of sight of land, are safe to eat, whereas some of the fish caught in lagoons may not only be poisonous to eat but poisonous to handle (see paras. 52 to 54).

49.   The flesh of fish is valuable food, but remember that it can be included in your diet only when you have sufficient water for its digestion, roughly two parts of water to one of fish.

50.   If you have more fish than you require, it can be dried in the sun for future use. This will probably make it more palatable, but dried fish, flesh, or entrails should not be eaten unless your water ration is at least 30 ounces per day.

51.   *Fishing—Useful Hints.*

    (a) Do not handle the fishing line with bare hands or fasten it to the dinghy. Use gloves or a cloth when handling fish, for even non-poisonous fish may have extremely sharp fins or gill covers.

    (b) If using a spoon or spinner, keep it moving, either by casting out and retrieving hand over hand, or by letting it down as far as the line will allow and again retrieving it, or by jigging at various depths.

    (c) Having caught a fish, you can cut its skin or flesh into strips with which to bait the hooks or spinners. The eyes and entrails also make good bait.

    (d) Do not fish in or near large shoals, as large fish (*e.g.* shark or barracuda) may be feeding from them.

    (e) A light at night attracts fish and is therefore an aid to fishing.

    (f) Surplus fish can be cut into strips and dried for future use as food or bait. It should last a few days.

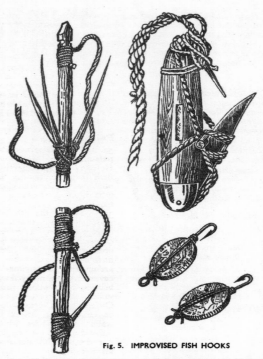

Fig. 5. IMPROVISED FISH HOOKS

(g) A dinghy often attracts small fish, which make excellent
bait. A dip net can be improvised in order to catch them.
If they can be caught in sufficient quantities these small
fish also make excellent food.

(h) A piece of cloth or wool, especially if it is red in colour, is a good substitute for bait. A tuft of hair or a white feather tied to the shank of the hook will often serve the same purpose. Some improvised fish hooks are illustrated in Figs. 5 and 6.

Poisonous Fish

52. Most fish are edible, palatable, and wholesome. However, there are a few with flesh that is poisonous and others with poisonous spines which are dangerous to handle.

53. Most of the fish with poisonous flesh are to be found in tropical waters. Their chief characteristic is that they lack ordinary scales, and instead have either a naked skin, or are encased in a bony box-like covering, or are covered with bristles, spiny scales, strong sharp thorns, or spines. Others puff up like a balloon on being taken out of the water. If you are ashore, remember that cooking does not destroy the poisonous alkaloids in these fish. Finally never eat a fish that has slimy gills, sunken eyes, flabby flesh or skin, or an unpleasant odour. If on pressing the

Fig. 6. IMPROVISED FISH HOOKS

thumb against the fish it remains deeply dented, the fish is probably stale and should not be eaten. Good flesh should be firm and not slimy.

54. Fish which are dangerous to handle have sharp spines on their heads, tails, or fins. These spines may cause a burning or stinging, or even an agonizing pain which is out of all proportion to the apparent severity of the wound. The pain is caused by the venom injected by the spines, which in some cases can be very dangerous if not fatal. These fish are usually either yellowish-grey or black in colour, often having patches of red or orange that give them a mottled appearance. Avoid all types of jelly fish, rays that have a diamond shaped body and long tail, and sea snakes. Sea snakes should be fairly easily distinguished from eels because, unlike eels, they have long plates or scales covering their bodies and heads, and compressed flattened tails. Sea snakes are normally found only in inshore tropical waters (Figs. 4 and 7).

Seaweeds

55. Most seaweeds are edible and, either raw or cooked, form a valuable addition to your diet, providing your water ration is adequate, for they tend to make you thirsty. Seaweeds are found mainly in inshore waters, but some of the seaweeds floating on the open ocean are good to eat. The following simple rules should be observed :—

(a) Fresh, healthy specimens have no marked odour or flavour and are firm and smooth to the touch. If the plant is wilted and slimy and has a fishy smell, it is decaying and should not be eaten.

(b) Do not eat the threadlike or slender branched forms. They are not poisonous, but may contain irritating acids. You can detect this by crushing some with your hands, when the released acid will cause the plant to decay so rapidly that within five minutes it will give off an offensive odour.

(c) Inspect the seaweed for small, stinging organisms which may be living in it. Crabs, shrimps, and small fish are often found attached to the seaweed and can be shaken off into the dinghy.

SCORPION FISH

PORQUPINE FISH

TOADFISH

STONEFISH

FILEFISH

STINGRAY

ZEBRA FISH

Fig. 7. POISONOUS AND VENOMOUS FISH

Birds

56. All sea birds are edible, either raw or cooked, though some may taste a little peculiar. They are scarce in the open ocean, more than 100 miles from land. The most characteristic of the ocean birds are the albatross, with a wing span of from six to twelve feet, and the petrel and hooked-beaked shearwater, which are about the size of a large pigeon. They can be caught, although not easily, by trolling a floating bait. A large fish hook could be used, but a gorge in the shape of a diamond, about four inches by one inch or more, floating on the surface, and completely covered by fish as bait, is probably more successful. The bird gets the gorge wedged in its throat after swallowing the bait (Fig. 8).

MAKING A LANDFALL

57. *Introduction.* The chances are odds-on that you will be found and rescued within four or five days. In time of war, sailing dinghies are used to enable ditched crews to head out to sea if they are uncomfortably close to an enemy held coastline. In peacetime, however, as has already been stated, you should put out the drogue and stay near the scene of ditching as long as possible. This will help the aircraft searching for you and increase the chance of your eventual rescue. However, you may have ditched in a remote part of the ocean where air and sea search is sparse, and this, together with other conditions, such as favourable trade winds or ocean currents, may ultimately lead you to try to make a landfall. The details of jungle desert, and arctic survival are dealt with in the other pamphlets of this series, but somewhat special conditions apply to the dry islands and atolls of the Indo-Pacific ocean area, where a landfall may be made (see paras. 62 to 63). These dry islands, as the name suggests, are islands where the rainfall is insufficient for normal vegetation, but where men can at least rest before continuing their journey, or even exist if necessary until rescued.

Fig. 8. OCEAN BIRDS

Petrel

Shearwater

Sooty Tern

Tropic (Bos'n) Bird

58. *Wind and Currents*. The movement of the dinghy will be mainly governed by the prevailing winds and ocean currents, and these can be utilized intelligently to make a landfall. The following points should be borne in mind :—

(a) The lower the dinghy rides in the water, and the lower its occupants sit or lie, the greater will be the effect of the current. This effect can be increased by the use of the drogue.

(b) On the other hand, if the wind is favourable the dinghy should be lightened as much as possible. Survivors should sit as erect as possible to increase the wind effect, and any sort of makeshift sail will help. The drogue should be hauled inboard, and the water ballast pockets tripped.

59. *Navigation and Direction at Sea*. If you are in a large dinghy with the remainder of your crew, and have your navigation equipment with you, so much the better. However, you may be alone, or without navigation equipment. If so, the following hints will help you to determine and maintain your course towards land or the shipping lanes :—

(a) If you have no compass, remember that the sun rises approximately in the east and sets in the west. If you are north of latitude 23½ deg. N., the sun will pass to the *south* of you in its path across the sky. South of latitude 23½ deg. S. it will pass to the *north* of you. Between these latitudes the sun's path varies with the time of year. The direction in which the sun rises is shown in the table below.

SUNRISE TABLE

DIRECTION IN WHICH SUN RISES — DEGREES EAST OF TRUE NORTH

Direction measured when top of sun just shows above horizon

Latitude	Mar. 21	May 5	June 22	Aug. 9	Sept. 23	Nov. 7	Dec. 22	Feb. 5
60° North ..	89°	55°	37°	55°	89°	122°	140°	122°
30° North ..	90°	71°	63°	71°	90°	108°	116°	108°
0° (Equator) ..	90°	74°	67°	74°	90°	106°	113°	106°
30° South ..	90°	72°	64°	72°	90°	104°	117°	109°

(b) Between sunrise and sunset, and north and south of the latitudes shown in the table, an approximate indication of direction can be obtained by using a watch. Point the hour hand at the sun, and a point on the watch dial halfway between the hour hand and twelve o'clock will indicate the approximate direction of true south if you are in the northern hemisphere, or of true north if you are in the southern hemisphere. In the tropics the method is unreliable.

(c) At night, if the sky is clear, reliable indications of direction can be obtained from the stars. In the northern hemisphere, true north can be ascertained from the constellation of the Great Bear, which points to Polaris (North Star), the star over the north pole. In the southern hemisphere, the Southern Cross indicates the direction of south. Other constellations, such as Orion, rise in the east and set in the west, moving to the south of you when you are north of the equator and *vice versa*. (See Figs. 9 to 11.)

(d) Trying to estimate your latitude by measuring the angle of Polaris above the horizon will give you only a very approximate result unless you have a sextant and tables, for even if you were able to estimate the angle to within five degrees you could still be 300 nautical miles in error.

(e) Between the equatorial belt of very light and variable winds, known as the "Doldrums", and the latitudes 30 deg. N. and 30 deg. S., the prevailing winds are the north-east and south-east trades respectively. These winds are a boon to navigation, being very steady both in direction and speed, although they are subject to certain seasonal variations. From latitude 40 deg. N. and S. towards the poles the winds are mainly westerly.

60. The above are only general hints. Learn as much as you can by observation and questions about the winds and sea currents in the areas in which you operate. Learn to pick out the stars that have been mentioned and many more. That is how the first navigators found their way, and without navigational instruments it is still the best.

61. *Land Indications.* Native fishermen whose small canoes are blown out to sea often turn up days later none the worse for their experience. They keep on with their fishing, catch birds, and quench their thirst with rain water caught during the frequent

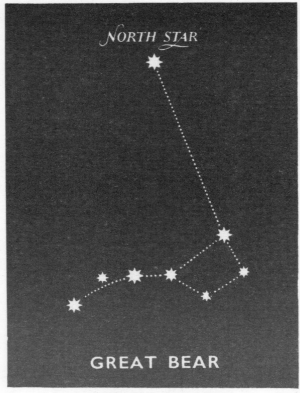

GREAT BEAR

Fig. 9. GREAT BEAR AND NORTH STAR

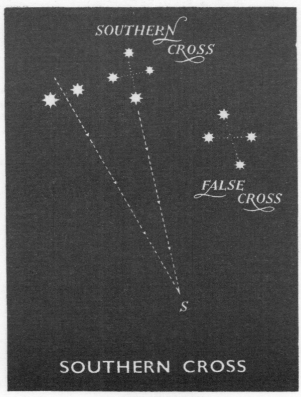

SOUTHERN CROSS

FALSE CROSS

SOUTHERN CROSS

Fig. 10. SOUTHERN CROSS

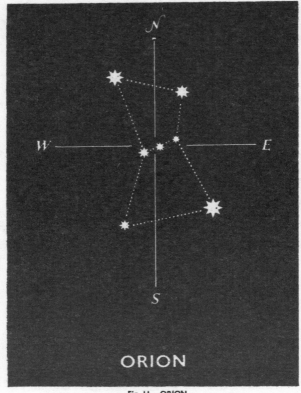

ORION

Fig. 11. ORION

squalls. They often detect the presence of an island long before it can be seen, by one of the following methods :—

(a) Cumulus clouds in an otherwise clear sky are likely to have been formed over land.

(b) Very few sea birds sleep on the water, and very rarely do they fly more than 100 miles from land. The recognition of these birds and their direction of flight will often indicate the direction and distance of land. They fly away from land before noon and return in the late afternoon and evening. Storms sometimes blow land-based birds far out to sea, so that a lone bird is not a reliable indication.

(c) Lagoon glare ; a greenish tint in the sky or on the under-side of a cloud caused by the reflection of sunlight from the shallow water over coral reefs.

(d) Drifting wood or vegetation is often a sign of the proximity of land.

LIVING ON LAND

62. *Water.* Many islands in the Indo-Pacific area have a good water supply, while others do not. On a dry island, water fit to drink can be obtained by digging a hole in a depression about 100 yards above the high tide mark. The water may be brackish, so go no deeper than is necessary : normally it will be sufficient to dig a foot deeper after the first water starts to seep through. The fresh water, being less dense, will float on top, so " skim " off the fresher water from the top of your well with a shell. Large scallop-type shells will also be found useful in digging the well. If the water is very brackish, try a new hole somewhere else. Even brackish water in very limited quantities will not sicken you, and will help to keep you alive. When you have dug a suitable well, line the hole with coral slabs or pieces of rock to prevent the sand from caving in.

63. *Food on Dry Islands.* Seafood is the principal source of food on the dry islands of the Indo-Pacific area. Rats are usually the only mammals found on them, and edible vegetation is limited to one or two species. A list of the various foods is given below.

(a) *Seafood.* Look for clams, mussels, sea cucumbers, crabs, crayfish, shrimps, and sea urchins. They will be found along the shore and in pockets formed by the coral reefs (see Figs. 12 and 13). Beware of the poisonous varieties of shellfish, with cone-shaped or pointed spindle-shaped shells. Shellfish can be eaten raw, but it is safer to

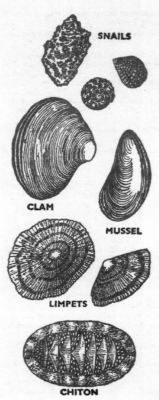

SNAILS

CLAM

MUSSEL

LIMPETS

CHITON

Fig. 12. EDIBLE SEAFOOD

cook them. One very simple way is to cover them with sand or earth and build a fire over the pile, when they will cook in their own juices. Another way is to drop them into boiling water.

(b) *Fish.* Fishing with hook and line has been dealt with in para. 51. Fish can often be found in pools on reefs or among rocks at low tide. If there are no natural pools on the reefs, try a fish trap. Fig. 14 shows two types of fish traps. In the maze type the trap should be about 8 feet across with a mouth about $1\frac{1}{2}$ feet wide, through which walls project two feet into the trap. It can be built with stones or stakes of wood. Fish that enter seldom find their way out.

(c) *Turtles.* Turtles breed on sandy shores and on small islands. They are all edible and their eggs are also an excellent source of nourishment. Follow the obvious trails made

SEA URCHIN

SEA CUCUMBER

SCALLOP

STAR FISH

Fig. 13. EDIBLE SEAFOOD

221

by sea turtles across the beach to find the places where the eggs are buried in the sand. When you have roughly determined the location of the eggs, prod the sand with a stick. Turtle eggs may be buried two feet deep and at a distance of about 20 yards from the water. They may be eaten raw but are much better boiled, although the white part remains watery. While spoiled eggs are to be avoided, those in an advanced state of incubation may be eaten if necessary. Turtles may be caught on the beach or on a reef. Rush them and turn them on their backs, but be careful of their jaws and claws. The neck can be pulled out and the throat cut or the entire head severed. Turtles are cleaned more easily after partial boiling or after cooking in a ground oven. Turtle steak and soup are luxuries and the blood is good food.

(d) *Pigweed or Purslane.* On barren atolls, the only readily edible vegetable food is the pigweed, a fleshy, soft-stemmed, reddish-green weed with yellow flowers, which stands 8 to 12 inches high and grows in large patches (see Fig. 15). It will relieve thirst, and tastes like watercress when eaten fresh and like slightly sour spinach when cooked. A diet of this plant, augmented by seafood, will sustain one indefinitely.

(e) *Pandanus or Screw Pine.* Less barren islands, having more soil and moisture, often support coconut palms and pandanus. The pandanus tree may be recognized by its palmlike trunk, heads of long spiny leaves, and aerial roots (see Fig. 16). The tender white flesh in the base of a head of young leaves may be eaten raw or cooked. The fruit, similar in size and appearance to the pineapple, is composed of segments or cones fixed to a soft core from

 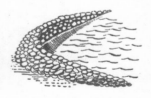

MAZE TYPE FISH TRAP   TIDAL FLAT FISH TRAP

Fig. 14. FISH TRAPS

which they readily separate when ripe. The ripe cones are orange yellow and very fragrant. Between the fibres and the soft inner part of the cones is lodged sugar and starch which may be extracted by chewing. After baking or roasting, scrape out the pulp with a shell or knife. The yellow paste can be eaten immediately or preserved by drying. The fruit is in season from June to October south of the equator. During the off season, the outer sides of the dry cones contain delicious kernels, which are lodged in small compartments in a hard shell. Cut off the fibrous end of the cone and place it on a flat rock, then crack it with a heavy stone held in both hands. Water can be obtained by tapping the tops of the aerial roots.

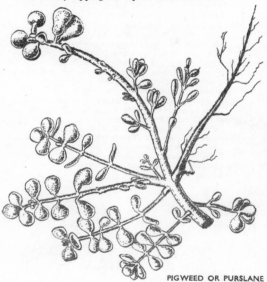

PIGWEED OR PURSLANE

Fig. 15

(f) Coconuts and the Coconut Palm. The coconut palm may be found on the less barren atolls, and is an ample provider of food. Each tree has nuts in all stages of growth. The green or yellowish-brown nuts contain excellent " milk " and " meat". You can attempt to climb the tree in your bare feet using the rough rings of the bark as steps, or by tying a piece of cloth between your ankles

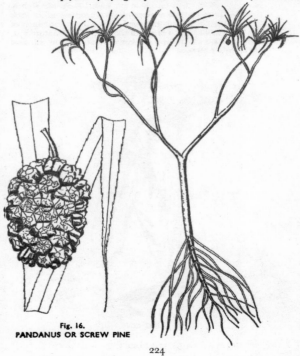

Fig. 16.
PANDANUS OR SCREW PINE

as a climbing bandage and hitching up the tree. Mature nuts can be picked up from the ground and are good to eat providing you can hear the milk inside when you shake them. The fibrous husk of the mature coconut can be prised off with a machete, but a husking stick of hard wood will do the job much better (see Fig. 17). To open a nut for drinking, pare off the soft outer shell at the pointed end with a machete or knife, then tap lightly around the end until a piece of hard shell about an inch or more in diameter is removed. Do not eat too much of the meat or drink too much of the milk of the mature nut, especially if you are in a weakened state, for you will find them very laxative.

Fig. 17. BREAKING COCONUTS

9/52 E43309/43693 Wt. 14965-BN.3592 10,800 12/53 Gp.8 F. & C. Ltd.

Notes

Notes

Notes

Notes

Notes

Notes

Notes

....
....
....
....
....
....
....
....
....
....
....
....
....
....
....
....
....
....
....
....